An Instrument in God's Hand

An Eye Surgeon's Discovery of the Miraculous

by

Elizabeth R. ⒢ D.

All Scripture references are from the Authorized King James Version of the Bible, unless otherwise indicated. References marked NAS are from the New American Standard Bible, Copyright © 1960, 1962, 1963, 1968, 1971, 1972, 1973, 1977 by the Lockman Foundation, La Habra, California. References marked AMPLIFIED are from the Amplified Bible, Copyright © 1987 by the Zondervan Corporation and the Lockman Foundation, La Habra, California.

McDougal Publishing is a ministry of The McDougal Foundation, Inc., a Maryland nonprofit corporation dedicated to spreading the Gospel of the Lord Jesus Christ to as many people as possible in the shortest possible time.

Published by:

McDougal Publishing
P.O. Box 3595
Hagerstown, MD 21742-3595

ISBN 1-58158-000-2

Printed in the United States of America
For Worldwide Distribution

There is really no limit to what God can do with a person, providing that one will not touch the glory. God is still waiting for one who will be more fully devoted to Him than any who has ever lived; who will be willing to be nothing that Christ may be all; who will grasp God's own purposes and taking His humility and His faith, His love and His power — without hindering, let God do great things.   Kathryn Kuhlman

(from a letter to Dr. Vaughan dated January, 1975)

Contents

Index of Photos

Foreword by Dino Kartsonakis

At the end of one of my concerts, I was privileged to meet Dr. Elizabeth Vaughan. I was aware of her expertise in eye surgery and the fact that she had been instrumental in bringing the technique of eye correction called keratotomy to the United States. She asked me the question, "How is your eyesight?" In a matter of days I was receiving the gift of healing for my own eyes.

Dr. Vaughan's credibility was so evident that I had great faith and security in knowing I was in good hands. As she follows God's leadership from His Word, she not only uses her instruments of healing for the eyes, SHE IS AN INSTRUMENT used of God in the service of His Kingdom.

Dr. Vaughan has become a dear friend to Cheryl and me, and we have been blessed as we continue to become even more aware of her generosity and sensitivity and as we have watched her share, in so many ways, the gift God has given her. As you read this book, may you be inspired and encouraged to become *An Instrument in God's Hand.*

Thank you, Dr. Vaughan, not only for the improvement of my eyesight, but for the example of commitment you have exemplified in helping people here at home and around the world.

Dino Kartsonakis

Foreword by Ruth Ward Heflin

Some readers may have heard Dr. Elizabeth Vaughan teaching the Word of God on her daily radio program "The End Crowd" or seen her ministering nightly on her telecast "Dr. Vaughan Presents." I first met her at the altar of St. Peter-en-Gallicantu where we conducted services for many years in Jerusalem. It was November of 1979.

Dr. Vaughan looked so familiar to me that I said to her, "I know you." She didn't think so because she had never been to the church before, but after I had thought about it a minute, I remembered where I had seen her.

"About a year ago," I said, "I saw a video of a Phil Donahue Show, and you were on that show. You're an eye doctor, and you were on with Brother R. W. Schambach to verify the miraculous healing of Ronald Cohen's eye."

She smiled and said, "Well, I guess you do know me."

At the time I met Dr. Vaughan in Jerusalem, we were in the process of trying to obtain visas in order to place a ministry team in China. It had been a slow process, and many of our team members were becoming weary of the waiting. I had been asking the Lord what He wanted us to do concerning the visas, and He spoke to me and said, "On Thanksgiving Day, you will have something to be thankful for."

I invited Dr. Vaughan to be the guest speaker at our meeting the following day, the Saturday before Thanksgiving, and I asked God to speak to me through her message that morning. She titled her message "Walk on the Water." It was a step-by-step story of how she had built and established a television station in Dallas, Texas. I knew

God was telling me to take a step of faith concerning the visas for China, to walk on water, as it were. I immediately went to our travel agent and booked a flight to Hong Kong with a stopover in Los Angeles.

Soon after I arrived in Los Angeles, we received word that the long-awaited visas had been granted, and the following day we left for Hong Kong, where we were able to obtain the necessary entry permits. We were the first such Christian group to have this great opportunity.

After processing all the necessary papers, we arrived back at our ministry house in Hong Kong in time to sit down together to a wonderful Thanksgiving meal. It was as the Lord had said. We truly did have something to be thankful for on Thanksgiving Day.

Dr. Vaughan was a big part of that China miracle and has been my friend ever since. Now you will come to know her through her book , *An Instrument in God's Hand.* You will see the process that God used to bring her to her present-day effectiveness in His service.

Short and petite, Dr. Vaughan's stature belies her great strength of soul and spirit. Since I have known her, I can say that her eye has always been single toward God and His Kingdom, and through the years, her vision has only enlarged and increased. She will surely be one of the great end-time players on God's stage of the miraculous.

Ruth Ward Heflin
Ashland, Virginia

Author's Preface

On my desk, I have a Chinese marble egg with a variety of bright colors intertwined in it. This book reminds me of that egg because it, too, has a variety of intertwined bright themes — from Kathryn Kuhlman to surgical instruments and worldwide travel experiences (especially China and Israel); from dreams and visions God has given me, to life-impacting lessons from the Word of God taught to me as only the Holy Spirit can teach.

I will share with you how my life was transformed from a nominal Christian who had no personal relationship with Jesus Christ into someone who walks and talks with Him throughout every day and watches Him do miracles in abundance. Above all, as you read this book, I want you to see how YOU can be *An Instrument in God's Hand* in these end times.

Introduction

It was a hot summer day in Cincinnati in 1993. For me, it was a very special day because it was my birthday.

I was praying for sick people at the altar of a local church, where I had been holding a revival, when a lady approached me and asked if I would come back and pray for her sister who, she said, was unable to come to the front. Without hesitating and without thinking, I followed her.

She led me halfway back in the auditorium to an aisle seat, where her sister was sitting, a walker by her side. I said to her, "Rise, in the name of Jesus, and be healed." I had no idea what her problem was. That never entered my mind. I simply took her by the arm, lifted her to her feet, and the two of us began walking down the center aisle of the church together.

I say "walking," but the truth is that she was laboriously shuffling along, taking tiny baby steps. I noticed that the arm I was holding was very stiff. In fact, her entire body seemed stiff and immobile. None of these facts deterred me from encouraging her to walk.

Then, suddenly, a miraculous thing happened. The arm I was holding made a popping sound, and so did other parts of her body. I felt the arm become more flexible. This must have simultaneously happened in her legs because she began taking better steps.

By this time, we had arrived at the altar, and I proceeded to walk with her across the front of the church building — once, then twice — and each time she was able to walk faster, until her shuffle became actual steps.

The third time we crossed the front of the altar area, we were jogging together, and I realized that she was going faster than I was.

I let go of her arm, and she took off running with all her might. She ran down the side aisle to the back of the church and then across the back. She was running like an Olympic sprinter.

She came down the center aisle like she was doing the hundred-yard dash. I had never seen anyone run so fast in my life. She was running so fast, in fact, that when she got to the altar area, there was no way she could make the turn. She didn't seem to care. Just where the center aisle ended, she slid under the altar, like a baseball player sliding into home plate and laid there under the power of God.

All of us who had witnessed the event stood there in shock. A woman as stiff as a board had suddenly turned into a gazelle as she was healed by the power of God.

After the service, the pastor told me the woman's story. He and his family had gone to a local restaurant and had just ordered their food when they looked out the window and saw this lady struggling to get out of a car. She worked her feet out first and then, grimacing with pain, she very slowly hoisted herself up onto her walker. Her feet moved only in tiny steps, and each tiny step seemed to take great effort and cause her excruciating pain.

The food arrived, and the family had finished eating and were already gathering their belongings and preparing to leave the restaurant by the time the lady and her sister, who accompanied her, were able to make it through the front door and to a table nearby. It had taken her more than thirty minutes to get inside and get seated.

Feeling great compassion for the woman, and recognizing that she desperately needed a miracle, the pastor spoke with her and her sister and told them about our revival meetings the following week. God would be doing miracles, he told them, and he hoped that they would attend. The lady answered that her doctors had done everything they knew to do, but were unable to help her further with her crippling disease. It was only after the pastor had encouraged them further that they had promised that they would try to come. Thank God they did.

How had a well-educated, scientifically trained medical doctor like me end up in a Cincinnati church, watching God do miracles? Allow me to take you back to the beginning and share with you, through the pages of this book, my discovery of the miraculous.

Elizabeth R. Vaughan, M.D.
Eye Surgeon
Dallas, Texas

Part I:

The Foundations of My Life in Christ

Chapter 1

The Early Years

It had been a hot Arizona day, but it was now night, and a cool, gentle summer breeze was blowing in through the second-story window of my grandparents' house, where I was staying. Every summer I would spend two weeks with them in Phoenix. At bedtime, Grandmother would read me Bible stories, then kiss me good-night and turn out the lights. I was then left alone with the gentle breeze, thinking of the men she had read to me about: Daniel in the den with those ferocious lions or David killing the huge giant with a single stone. What a big God took care of them!

My grandfather had been a successful businessman in Alabama until he became very ill. After doctors told him that his only chance for survival was to move to an arid climate, he committed his life to God, became a Methodist minister and moved his family to the southwestern United States, there to live by faith. Many were the times my grandparents would sit their children down to an

At four years of age, wearing my uncle's navy hat.

At six.

empty dinner table and thank God for providing a meal when the cupboards were bare. Invariably, there would be a knock on the door as they still sat praying, and a parishioner would be standing there saying, "Here, Reverend, I brought you a chicken," or "Here are some vegetables from my garden." The everyday life of my grandparents was a walk of faith.

I can remember being allowed, as a small child, to ring the bells in Granddad's church. I would jump as high as I could and grab the rope that was attached to those big bells. Then, I would hang onto the rope with all my weight until the bells began to chime. I would continue ringing the bells until it was time for church to start.

I can also remember my grandfather crying as he preached. I never understood exactly why he was crying, but I was old enough to perceive that it had something to do with his love for the Lord.

My mother was devoted to God in the same way her parents had been. Every time the church doors opened, she had me there. I never missed Sunday school, even if we went out of town. Church was an integral part of our lives. I can remember cold winter nights when I would lie on the floor in front of the furnace, and Mother would read the Bible to me for hours until I finally fell asleep and was carried to my bed.

My father was a bighearted, witty man who lead an upright life and was diligent in supporting his family. His father had been a medical doctor. I was told he once swam the Mississippi River to take care of a patient on the other side. My grandfather died the year I was born, so I never knew him, but I have his Bible. He made marginal notes throughout, and this has always indicated to me that he was a man who loved the Word of God.

When I was seven, I decided that I was old enough to be accountable to God for all my actions. Six, I supposed, was really too young to be accountable, and I was sure that God would have forgiven me for anything wrong I had done until then. Now that I was seven, however, I was surely old enough to be held responsible, and I would have to live right. I stayed in church faithfully as I grew up, becoming a youth leader and president of the Methodist Youth Fellowship.

As I grew older, of course, so did my grandparents. My grandfather became quite ill while I was in college, and I went to visit him for what would be the last time. During that visit, he said to me, "You will be a medical missionary one day." I respected my grandfather greatly and would never have contradicted him, but in my heart I wondered how that prediction could ever come true. Yes, I was a pre-med student at the time, but I was caught up in my studies and in the campus activities. I had no thoughts of being a missionary. Evidently God had given my grandfather a glimpse of things to come far beyond my own current vision, and he had spoken them prophetically over me.

My parents.

Grandmother lived for a few more years, becoming quite feeble in her late eighties. I asked her one day if she would rather stay on Earth or go to Heaven. Her answer made a lasting impression on me. She said, "Wherever the Lord wants me, that's where I want to be." She had no will of her own, but only wanted God's will to be done in her life. At her funeral, as I reflected over the early years of my life, I was filled with gratitude for a godly heritage. It was a profound blessing that I had been born into such a family, and I vowed to pass on the blessings they had left me. I had been given the gift of a strong foundation upon which I could build my life.

Mother taught me to pray.

Chapter 2

How God Led Me into Eye Surgery

I entered college as a math major because I liked mathematics very much. As I investigated careers in math, however, I discovered that I had two primary options. I could be a teacher, or I could get into the computer industry. Neither of these choices appealed to me, so I decided to go to the testing and counseling center at the college and take an aptitude test. I had heard that such a test could point me to appropriate career options.

For those who have never taken a test like this, I should explain. A series of questions is asked about the student's preferences. A sample question might go like this: "Which would you rather do — 1) Plant a garden, 2) Type a letter, or 3) Read a book?" The answers to many questions like this are tabulated, and the result usually suggests certain aptitudes.

When a counselor called me in to go over the test results, he explained that the test normally produced results in three categories: 1) Careers that you should seriously consider, 2) Careers that you might want to investigate, and 3) Careers for which you have no aptitude and which you should not consider. He was a bit apologetic as he began to address the specific results of my test. He said that he had never seen a test result quite like it in all his years of counseling students.

The evaluation of my test answers had produced only one option in the first category, nothing at all in the second, and everything else was in the third category. The only career in the first category was medicine. He tried not to be too strong in suggesting that I look into medicine, but there was nothing else to suggest.

I was shocked by the test results. Although one of my grandfathers had been a medical doctor, I had never considered medicine. Since no other aptitude had been suggested by the test results, I decided to investigate medicine as a career, so that summer I worked in a hospital. I found that I liked the work, and I, therefore, switched to being a pre-med major as a sophomore.

At the time I received the strange test results, I had no explanation for it. In retrospect, it is clear to me that the hand of the Lord was leading me in the way He wanted me to go. I cannot recall praying about the aptitude test or asking God for His guidance at that point in my life, but the episode clearly points out how He loves us and helps us before we really know Him and how He answers before we ever call on Him. Jesus is so very wonderful!

After graduating from the university and entering medical school, I began to ponder specialties within medicine. I had decided to do an internship in pediatrics after graduation. About halfway through this pediatric internship I realized that I did not want to spend the rest of my life practicing pediatrics, and I began to consider other possibilities.

We had not had much exposure to ophthalmology (eye surgery) in medical school, but what we did study had fascinated me, so I began to spend any spare time I had (which was very little) in the eye clinic. In the end, I decided I would like to make a career of ophthalmology. This was not an easy decision to implement because the residency programs in ophthalmology were much sought after and were filled up years in advance.

One day around Christmas of that year I happened to run into the head of the Ophthalmology Department in the cafeteria and mentioned to him that I would like to go into ophthalmology. He reconfirmed what I already knew — that the residency program that was to start in June of that next year had been filled up for a long time. It was interesting, he said, that I had spoken to him that day because he had just gotten notification that one of the doctors scheduled to start the program that June had been drafted into the military. That opened one spot, and the members of the committee making those decisions were going to have to pull out the long list of those who had applied and choose another doctor to fill the vacancy. He would accept my application, he told me, and put me up for consideration along with all the rest.

Consideration for the residency, of course, would require a thorough review of the transcript of my grades from medical school and a series of personal interviews with the staff, among other things. When the process was finished, much to my joy, I was selected for the one open slot, and I began my residency (specialty training) in ophthalmology.

Again, I see the hand of Jesus in all this. I only wish that I could have recognized it sooner and given Him glory earlier in my life. At the time, I somehow felt that I had "a little pink cloud" over my head that made things turn out wonderful for me over and over. Now I know that there is no such thing. What happened to me that enabled me to enter medicine in general and ophthalmology in particular is nothing more than the unmerited favor of God.

His daily favor upon my life is still unmerited, but now, at least, it is recognized and treasured. I have come to understand what Jesus meant when He told Paul, *"My grace* [unmerited favor] *is sufficient for thee"* (2 Corinthians 12:9). If we have God's favor, there is truly nothing else in life that we need.

Chapter 3

The First Step in the Spirit

By 1973 I had finished four years of University, four years of medical school, a year of internship, three years of residency training in Ophthalmology, and had been in medical practice for three years as an eye surgeon. One day a young man who was a patient asked if I could help support him financially as he worked full-time with

During my college days.

Campus Crusade for Christ. I agreed to help and subsequently began getting literature from that organization.

A flier from Campus Crusade for Christ came in the mail one day announcing a "spiritual enrichment" retreat at Lake Texoma. I was attending the Methodist church, my practice of medicine was already successful, I had a nice car, a nice house and everything else I wanted. I decided, however, that I probably could use some spiritual enriching, so I signed up for the retreat.

At that retreat, I heard the testimony of a man from Chicago who owned warehouses. He had been careful to tithe from his business, and it had flourished. As he became more heavily involved in ministry, he decided to sell the warehouses so that he could have more time to dedicate to the work of God. The people who bought the business from him did not tithe as he had been doing, and gradually their business declined.

A large motorcycle dealership account moved its business to another warehouse, and others followed. The new owners did everything they could think of to keep their customers and to attract new business, but things continued to grow worse. They became so desperate that one day they called the previous owner to ask him to attend one of their board meetings and give them suggestions about what they were doing wrong.

At that meeting, the man listened carefully to the plight of these new owners. When he was given an opportunity to speak, he asked if they were continuing to tithe from the business. They answered that they could not afford to tithe and had stopped the practice long ago. He suggested that they all get on their knees, commit their lives to Christ, and promise God to tithe on every dollar they made from that moment on. Desperate situations require desperate actions.

Since the new owners were in imminent danger of losing everything, they acted on this suggestion. After that night of prayer and commitment, they were faithful to tithe over the coming days and weeks, and things began to improve. Someone from the motorcycle dealership called to say that the other warehouse had damaged some of their vehicles, so they wanted to move their account back. The business quickly grew and flourished once again, because God was being honored.

That testimony from a businessman impacted my life. I had heard many pastors talk about Jesus, but here was an ordinary layperson who had a vibrant walk with his Master. I went away from there convinced that there must be a lot more of God available for me that I knew nothing about.

I was given a little booklet at that retreat called "The Four Spiritual Laws." In it, there was a diagram showing a person's life as a circle with a throne in the center. When self was on the throne (in control of one's life), the life contained frustration, hostility, anger, discouragement and many other undesirable characteristics. When Jesus was on the throne and ruled that life, it grew love, joy, peace, patience, goodness, gentleness and faith. When I compared the fruits of the two lives, there was no question which one I wanted to have. I immediately fell on my knees and said, "Lord, I have made mistakes, but whatever is left of this life, I ask You to take it and use it for Your purposes." I gave my life to Jesus that day with a new understanding. How could I have been in church all those years and not known I could literally GIVE my life to Jesus?

Having made a serious commitment, I decided I must put feet to my decision. I knew what Jesus had said:

> *Seek ye first the kingdom of God, and His righteousness; and all these things* [food, drink, clothes, etc.] *shall be added unto you.*
> Matthew 6:33

I decided to do it, to seek Him with all my heart. But how could I do this? I knew that God honors His Word above His name, so I decided to dig into the Word (the Bible) in a serious way. I began setting my alarm to wake up thirty minutes earlier than usual in order to have time to study the Word.

My time with the Word of God turned out to be so exciting that I hated for the thirty minutes to end. I decided to set my alarm for an hour earlier than I was accustomed to rising, and the exact same thing happened. I was, again, so disappointed when the hour was over that I started setting my alarm for an hour and a half earlier than normal. This progression continued until I was getting up at almost the same time I was going to bed.

I found the Word of God to be alive, real and exciting! I fell in love with it and wanted to know it all — every tiny detail. I also wanted to DO it all, to experience it all. I wanted to consume it and be consumed by it. I wanted to be ONE with it.

I also received some little booklets from Campus Crusade for Christ called *The Nine Transferable Concepts.* One of those booklets was about being filled with the Holy Spirit, and in it was a quotation from St. Luke:

> *If a son shall ask bread of any of you that is a father, will he give him a stone? or if he ask a fish, will he for a fish give him a serpent? Or if he shall ask an egg, will he offer him a scorpion? If ye then, being evil, know how to give good gifts unto your children: how much more shall your heavenly Father give the Holy Spirit to them that ask him?*   Luke 11:11-13

That was enough for me. If God said He would give the Holy Spirit to whoever asked, then I was going to ask. I knelt in my living room alone and asked to be filled with the Holy Spirit. I saw no vision and heard no voice, yet I knew I had been filled with the Spirit because the Word of God said so. I received the Spirit by faith, the same way a person is saved.

I really did not know much about the Holy Spirit at that time. I did not know, for instance, the term Jesus used: *"baptized with the Holy Ghost"* (Acts 1:5). I knew nothing about speaking in tongues, and none of the Christians I knew were aware of such things. But I had set my face like a flint to seek the Lord, and there is a law of God — *"Seek and ye shall find"* (Luke 11:9) — and find I did!

I asked God to send me a friend who knew more about the things of the Holy Spirit, and He did. Soon, a whole new world was opened to me.

My new friend began taking me to church meetings and other meetings where the Holy Spirit was completely free to move as He chose. One evening she took me to a meeting in a large and lovely home, where a visiting pastor was going to be ministering. About thirty people were in attendance, seated leisurely around the periphery of the living room, like in a home fellowship group. The pastor brought a stirring message and then began to pray for those with needs. Sometimes God would give a message to some individual through the pastor. I later learned that this is one of the gifts that the Holy Spirit gives to those who serve God.

> *But to each one is given the manifestation of the Spirit for the common good. For to one is given the word of wisdom through the Spirit, and to another the word of knowledge according to the same Spirit; to another faith by the same Spirit, and to another gifts of healing by the one Spirit, and to another the effecting of miracles, and to another prophecy, and to another the distinguishing of spirits, to another various kinds of tongues, and to another the interpretation of tongues. But one and the same Spirit works all these things, distributing to each one individually just as He wills.* 1 Corinthians 12:7-11, NAS

A woman stood up near me for prayer, and the pastor came over to her and began praying for her. As his hands were laid on her, she fell down on the floor right by my feet. I was concerned. Was she unconscious? Was she dead? As a medical doctor, I wanted to jump up and give her CPR, but I noticed that everyone else in the room seemed totally unconcerned about this woman being "out" like this on the floor. The pastor calmly stepped over her and went on praying for others, like nothing had happened.

What should I do? I wondered. I decided to watch her breath, and as long as she was breathing I would not be too alarmed. After quite a while, the lady got up and took her seat.

What on earth was going on? I was wondering. If I had known my Bible better at the time, I would not have been so shocked. After all, when Judas and the band of men with him came to lay hold of Jesus, something very similar happened:

> *Jesus ... said unto them, Whom seek ye?*
> *They answered him, Jesus of Nazareth.*
> *Jesus saith unto them, I am he. And Judas also, which betrayed*
> *him, stood with them. As soon then as he had said unto them, I*
> *am he, they went backward, and fell to the ground.*
>
> John 18:4-6

Coming into the presence of the Son of the living God had been an experience that overwhelmed the bodies of these men, and they fell backwards onto the ground. Since we know that Jesus Christ is just *"the same yesterday, and to day, and for ever"* (Hebrews 13:8), why should we be surprised when coming into His powerful presence today elicits the same response in our bodies as it did in these men two thousand years ago?

Nevertheless, when I first saw this happen, I was totally shocked. Now, as the Spirit is being poured out to an even greater extent in this present age, we see this phenomenon happening all around us and even view it on television. It is commonly referred to as "being slain in the Spirit." It is a very real experience. God is *"no respecter of persons"* (Acts 10:34), and He allows this experience to come to saints and sinners alike as they come into His overpowering presence.

Often, while a person is thus "slain in the Spirit," the Lord will speak to them or drastically change their life, as they are lying on the floor. His presence is never to be feared if we are His children. Being in the presence of Jesus is more precious than any other experience in life — whether it happens while you are on your knees, standing on your feet, or lying on your back under His power.

I was learning things that would change my life forever.

Part II:

Being an Instrument in God's Hand

Chapter 4

A Gift for Kathryn Kuhlman

Not long after this I came to know about the amazing woman of faith, Kathryn Kuhlman. She came to Dallas, Texas, to hold meetings for the Full Gospel Business Men. Her meetings were like stepping into a higher realm in God, like stepping into a heavenly cloud of His presence. There was a quiet reverence in her services, as thousands of people of every background were unified in the worship of Jesus.

Miss Kuhlman's words were so powerful that we could hardly wait to hear what she would say next. Deep waters were flowing out of her, and these waters were bringing life and liberty to those of us in attendance.

I will never forget Kathryn Kuhlman speaking to us about dying to self, dying to self-will or "flesh," so that Jesus could become the sole Person in control of our lives. She walked to the edge of the stage and slowly peered over it, as if looking into a coffin. Then she said, "You can say anything you want to a dead man, and he won't blink an eye."

When the Holy Spirit speaks through a person, we remember the content of His words all the rest of our lives, and that is what happened to many of us through Kathryn Kuhlman.

Christmas was approaching, and I asked the Lord to show me a special gift I could send to Miss Kuhlman that would be meaning-

The framed forceps given to Kathryn Kuhlman

ful to her spiritually. I thought she probably had plenty of material things, and I was not interested in sending just another gift. I wanted to send her something that would bless her in a private way, a way that only Jesus knew about. Much to my surprise, He told me to send her my favorite, most useful, surgical instrument.

I could not do surgery without this particular instrument, so I ordered another one right away. I took the one I had been using for several years and mounted it in a gold picture-box frame. I did not want to send it to her without an explanation, but I did not know what the instrument meant, so I kept asking Him what I should say.

I had wanted her to have the gift by Christmas, but by Christmas Eve I still had no answer from the Lord, so I had no choice but to wait. On Christmas morning, at 4:00 a.m., I was awakened, and the Lord gave me the explanation. I got up and wrote the following letter:

A Gift for Kathryn Kuhlman

December 25, 1974

Dearest Kathryn:

I am writing early this Christmas morning because I want you to be the first person in this house to receive a present on our Lord's birthday. Three weeks ago I asked the Lord what you would like for Christmas that no one knew about, that would meet the desires of your heart. This 0.12 mm toothed forceps was His answer. Let me explain what it means.

For the last four-and-a-half years I have used this very instrument on every single cataract operation that the Lord and I have performed. It is indispensable to me. It has three teeth on the end that are 0.12 mm long. You will need some means of magnification to see these teeth well. They are used to grasp tissue so that a needle can be passed through it while it is being held with firmness but gentleness. The teeth must be perfectly aligned to grasp the tissue properly. If they are mal-aligned one hair's breadth, they might as well be thrown away, for they will no longer grasp in an exacting manner.

The reason this instrument and its function are so crucial is because it is used for closing the wound after a cataract has been removed. This means that the eye is wide open, and there is no margin for error in the surgeon or the instrument. If this instrument is not grasping properly, causing any pressure to be exerted on an open eye, the contents from inside the eye could be pressed out and the patient's vision compromised if not lost completely. All of this surgery is done through an operating microscope under high magnification. These forceps must grasp tissue 1/2 mm thick and hold it firmly enough to pass a needle through it, while exerting no pressure whatsoever on the open eye.

I love this precision instrument. It has served me well and been in the middle of many surgical miracles the Lord has performed. It has functioned perfectly for these four and a half years of use, and now I want you to have it on this Christmas morning. It is intended to serve as a reminder from our heavenly Father to you that this instrument has been in my hand like you are in His hand.

You are exactly what He wants you to be. He did not want you to be a pair of scissors or an instrument for extracting the cataract. He intended from the beginning of time for you to be a 0.12 mm toothed forceps holding the tissue so The Great Physician can do the stitching and healing.

Not many people in this world are so yielded that God can make of them exactly what He wants them to be, but you are. Our Father wants you to know, on His Son's birthday, that He loves you beyond words and that it gives Him great pleasure to have such a precision instrument as Kathryn Kuhlman available for Him to use as He wishes.

Amen and amen!

Dr. Vaughan

I was very happy about sending the instrument and the letter to Miss Kuhlman because I knew it was from God. All I wanted to do was bless her in some small way. She had blessed me and countless others in such a large way by being a yielded vessel. That January I was thrilled to receive a personal letter from Miss Kuhlman as follows:

January 8, 1975

Dear Dr. Vaughan:

The 'framed forcep' — your gift sent on Christmas Day — is standing on my desk for everyone to see, and as a continual reminder of the very precious things you wrote in your letter — I shall cherish it as long as I live!

There is really no limit to what God can do with a person, providing that one will not touch the glory. God is still waiting for one who will be more fully devoted to Him than any who has ever lived; who will be willing to be nothing that Christ may be all; who will grasp God's own purposes and taking His humility and His faith, His love and His power — without hindering, let God do great things.
MAY WE BOTH CONTINUE TO BE INSTRUMENTS IN HIS HAND!

Kathryn Kuhlman

Imagine, God is still waiting for one who will be more fully devoted to Him than anyone who has ever lived. That includes Moses and David, Peter and Paul, all the consecrated saints of God throughout time, including Miss Kuhlman. Who will that one be? Will you be the one who is willing to be nothing so that Christ can be everything? Will you be the one who will let God do great things without hindering?

For my part, I was learning more every day about how to become an instrument in God's hand.

Chapter 5

Being an Available Instrument

Over the years, God has taught me many things through my surgical instruments. As an eye surgeon, I must use very delicate instruments that are placed on a sterile tray beside me in the operating room. All of these instruments are available for my use at any given time, should I need them. Some instruments are used in every case, while others are used infrequently.

A patient came in one day with an intraocular lens that had slipped out of place and fallen into a jellylike substance at the back

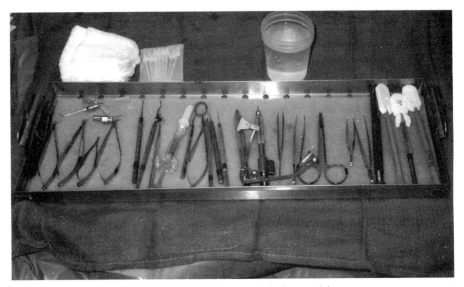

A tray of surgical instruments. Many kinds are needed.

of the eye known as vitreous. The lens was made of silicone, and I knew it would be very hard to grasp after it was coated with the slippery vitreous. None of the instruments I had would do the job. If I tried using ordinary instruments to retrieve the slippery lens, it would just squirt away and fall farther back into the vitreous, complicating things even more. What should I do?

A friend of mine who is a retinal surgeon had a special pair of forceps with small pieces of diamond on the tips that would bite down and hold tight onto any slippery lens, so I borrowed that special instrument just for this one surgical case.

While performing the required surgery, I reached carefully and slowly into the vitreous with this diamond-tipped instrument and gently grasped the lens. When I was sure I had a good grip on it, I held it firmly, as I slowly, but surely, removed it from the eye. I was then able to insert a new lens, one that would not slip, and the patient was able to see well again.

The thing to understand from this is that you may not be an instrument like a pastor or evangelist that people see God using every day. You may be a specialized instrument that is lying on the instrument tray waiting for the Great Physician to use you. But when He reaches for you, know that none other could take your place. You were made in a specific way for a specific purpose. God has molded you and shaped you according to His will to meet His needs.

Do not be discouraged if it seems that God is not using you all the time like someone else. He will use your mouth, your hands, and your loving heart. It is not necessary to be in "full-time ministry" to be used of God. He needs people in every walk of life, in every town, in every home.

We are all part of one body, and the eye cannot say to the ear, "I do not need you." We are all essential in our own function to make the whole body work. One part is not more important than another part. If someone has beautiful eyes, those eyes are no more important than the liver. In fact, the body could live without the pretty eyes, but would die without the liver.

The liver does not look very good; you do not think about it or talk about it, but it is an unseen member that is essential to life. So do not look at your pastor or evangelist (the pretty eyes) and feel you are not important (a liver cell) because you are not seen or heard. You may be an intercessor that is affecting nations by your prayer and no one knows about it but Jesus.

The Apostle Paul taught very clearly:

> *And the eye cannot say unto the hand, I have no need of thee: nor again the head to the feet, I have no need of you. Nay, much more those members of the body, which seem to be more feeble, are necessary: And those members of the body, which we think to be less honourable, upon these we bestow more abundant honour; and our uncomely parts have more abundant comeliness.*
>
> 1 Corinthians 12:21-23

I have known people who were sure God was going to use them, but they grew impatient waiting on Him and tried to accomplish the work on their own. Those who do this end up exhausted and frustrated because flesh cannot do what the Spirit can. These people remind me of a little bird in a cage that cannot stand the confinement, the limitation, the wait. If he grows too impatient, he may flap his wings with great vigor and start banging into the sides of the cage, destroying his own feathers, damaging his own wings and sapping all his energy. Then, when the door is opened, he is not able to fly out.

God spoke through Isaiah the prophet:

> *But they that WAIT upon the LORD shall renew their strength; they shall mount up with wings as eagles; they shall run, and not be weary; and they shall walk, and not faint.*
>
> Isaiah 40:31

If that little bird will just wait patiently until he has grown big enough and strong enough, until his master decides that the time is right and opens the door for him, then he can have all his feathers intact, his wings whole and the strength he needs to fly high.

If you are an instrument on God's tray, He is the one and the only one who decides when and how to use you. The decision is not yours. Leave it with Him.

From a surgeon's perspective, I can tell you that there are instruments I rarely use, but when I need them, I really need them! You may be an instrument just like that.

For instance, we use a little lens positioner. It has a long narrow shaft with a little mushroom-looking ball on the end of it. I rarely ask for it, but when I need it, nothing else will do. It must be on my tray, AVAILABLE to me at all times, and we must be available to God and must have no preconceived ideas about how He will use us. That is not our business; it is God's business.

How would it work if my forceps decided it wanted to be used like scissors, and it wanted it now, like some of us? How ludicrous! A forcep has no cutting edges. It has no cross-action movements. It was not designed to be used like scissors, and it would be impossible to use it like scissors. Still, many Christians decide how they want to be used by God, and they insist that He use them that way and NOW. If it does not happen their way, they are disappointed and frustrated and feel that they have failed God, or He has failed them. This is completely backwards. It is God's prerogative to decide how He wants to use us and when. Our job is simply to be available to Him.

I knew a man once who, after he had retired from his regular job, became the custodian of a certain church. He did a good job, and they came to depend on him. He was, however, quite dissatisfied. He wanted more than anything to be a preacher. He had no apparent gifts or anointing to preach, but that is what he (i.e., his flesh) wanted. This thought seemed to consume him, making him miserable every day and in every area of his life.

I always felt sad for this man who was making himself and those around him so miserable by desiring to be something he was never designed to be. He would have been so much happier if he could just have realized that God WAS using him. He could have been whistling a tune with a smile on his face at the privilege of taking care of God's house every day. He could have prayed over the sanctuary as he cleaned it. He could have been an uplifting force on every person that came through the church doors during the week. He could have been a powerful force for good in the life of that church simply by joyfully accepting his role in the Body of Christ.

We are much better off to blossom where we are planted and be diligent over what God puts in our hands. Rather than be constantly jealous of someone else's calling, let us be dedicated to our own. More importantly, let us be CONTENT. The Apostle Paul wrote:

> *For I have learned, in whatsoever state I am, therewith to be content.* Philippians 4:11

> *But godliness with contentment is great gain.* 1 Timothy 6:6

We are bondservants of Christ. We belong to our Master, and we have nothing because it all belongs to Him. We have given ourselves to Him, for His use. Our time is His. Our money is His. Our life is completely His. Whatever we do is to be done at His direction, not ours. We live for His pleasure.

> *For it is God which worketh in you both to will and to do of his good pleasure.* Philippians 2:13

As I think of availability, I am reminded of an incident that happened to me in China. I had taken surgical equipment, such as intraocular lenses and sutures and medicines, from Dallas to Beijing for use in my surgery cases there. The suitcase containing these items was entrusted to a young eye surgeon, Dr. Chin, and he was charged with its safekeeping. While in the middle of cataract surgery, I asked for an intraocular lens from the suitcase and was told that Dr. Chin had taken the suitcase to another building about a block away. I had to have that lens to finish the case, so I had to sit there and wait for someone to go find Dr. Chin and bring the lens to me. Finally someone arrived with the intraocular lens, and I was able to insert it into the patient's eye.

I was about to finish the case when I asked for a certain medicine I felt the patient needed to make the eye heal better. "Oh, Dr. Chin has it in the suitcase," I was told. I was shocked. I couldn't believe they would make this same mistake twice. Again I had to wait in the middle of my surgery for someone to go find Dr. Chin and bring the desired medicine. After that, I firmly instructed him to always keep that suitcase in surgery with me where its contents would be AVAILABLE for use as I needed them.

In the same way, of what usefulness is it to God, when He has carefully prepared someone as an instrument, if they are off somewhere doing their own thing, unavailable to Him, when He needs them? Make yourself available to the Great Physician. Put yourself on His tray of instruments, and let Him decide when and how to use you. Be happy with the glorious fact that you are on His tray. Be happy with the knowledge that He will use you according to His good pleasure. Be happy that you belong to Him.

Chapter 6

Being a Sterile Instrument

One day, as I was in the middle of surgery, the handle of my sterile instrument touched the microscope (which was not sterile). This contaminated the instrument, and I could no longer use it. If I had continued to use it, it would have contaminated my gloves, the other instruments and the eye on which I was operating. This could have caused an infection, which, in turn, could have caused the eye to

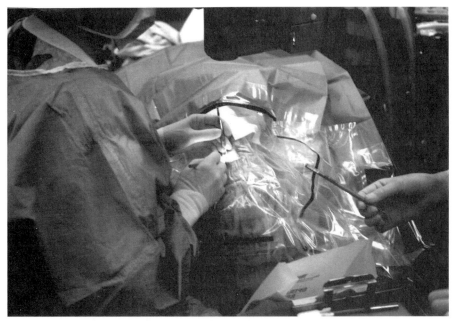

The toothed forceps being used in actual surgery.

go blind. I had to hand the instrument to the circulating nurse and ask her to re-sterilize it.

This instrument was just like a Christian who becomes spotted with sin. The contamination of sin prevents that person from staying in God's hand, but it is an easy thing to rectify. The Scriptures teach us:

> *If we confess our sins, he is faithful and just to forgive us our sins, and to cleanse us from all unrighteousness.* 1 John 1:9

Repenting, turning away from sin and asking God to forgive you, is like putting the instrument back in the sterilizer. When this short and quick process is complete, you come out sterile (free from sin), and you are ready once more for the Master's use.

The instrument that was contaminated in this case was one that I needed very badly to finish the surgery. I did not have another instrument on my tray that could have taken its place. While the instrument was being sterilized, therefore, I had to sit there with my hands folded and wait. While there was no way I could have waited long enough for the instrument company to make a new instrument and ship it to me, I could wait the few minutes it took for the sterilizer to do its work.

I wonder how many times God has had to fold His hands and wait for His people to ask for forgiveness, how many times He has had to stop His work and wait for us to be made clean by the blood of Jesus. It takes a lifetime for the Lord to mold us and shape us into just the specific instrument He needs. If that instrument becomes contaminated with sin, there is no replacement exactly like it. Must He start from scratch and make another instrument that can function in a similar way? What a sad thought!

God forbid that He should have to say, "You got dirty, and you chose to stay dirty. You made Me fold My hands the rest of your life."

How tragic that would be to force Jesus to say, *"Depart from Me, you who practice lawlessness"* (Matthew 7:23, NAS).

If you see yourself as a contaminated instrument today, please cry out for forgiveness now and become pure again so that the Lord can unfold His hands and proceed to use your life the way He has planned. Time is short, and He wants to use YOU. You are one of a kind. He has gone to a lot of trouble to make you just as you are. He made you that way because He needs you like that. No one can take your place, so apply the blood of Jesus to your sin and then quickly jump back onto the Lord's tray of instruments, available for His immediate use.

If you are willing to do this, when you see the Lord face to face in glory, He will be able to say to you:

> *Well done, thou good and faithful servant ... enter thou into the joy of thy Lord.*   Matthew 25:21

51

Chapter 7

Being an Instrument With No Will of Its Own

A man came to me one day for help. He had been in an industrial accident, and a piece of metal had penetrated his eye and was now in the middle of the vitreous (i.e., in the middle of the eye). He was taken to surgery right away where I made a small incision in the outer layers of the eye. Then I used a large magnet positioned over this incision to pull the piece of metal to it. The metal was thus removed, and the man's eye saved. We were all happy with the outcome.

The next time I did surgery I asked the nurse for the needle-holder to sew up an incision. Every time I tried to position the small metal needle correctly in the needle-holder, however, it suddenly seemed to have a mind of its own. It would snap onto the needle-holder in some strange position, and I had to try several times to get the needle positioned correctly. Each stitch I took presented the same problem over and over again.

It was a very aggravating situation, and it caused my work to be slower and more tedious. Apparently the needle-holder had touched the magnet during the previous emergency surgery and had become magnetized. It was "doing its own thing," and this was counterproductive to my doing what I needed to do.

I experienced that day a tiny glimpse into what it must be like for God to try to use us when we have a will of our own. He wants to do a certain thing, but He is hindered because we want to do it our way. Or, we have a preconceived idea of how we think God wants it, so we get busy doing it for Him. God does not need us to do His work for Him in our way. He needs yielded instruments, with no will of their own, with no preconceived ideas, with no hidden agendas.

Ideally, I think of us as being as dead to self as those metal instruments lying on the tray. They could never move on their own. They could never do surgery. In fact, they are really good for nothing unless a skilled surgeon picks one of them up and begins to use it in his or her hand. We can never accomplish God's will with our own efforts, any more than one of those instruments could do surgery without the surgeon. All we can do is crucify the flesh and be nothing. Then God can pick us up and use us however He chooses. Otherwise, we only cause interference:

> *Then Jesus said to His disciples, "If anyone desires to be My disciple, let him deny himself — that is, disregard, lose sight of and forget himself and his own interests — and take up his cross and follow Me."* Matthew 16:24, Amplified

Needless to say, I had to send that instrument away and get it demagnetized before I could use it again. It is almost impossible to use an instrument that has a will of its own. To be useful, a surgical instrument can only have one will, and that must be the will of the surgeon. After all, that instrument does not know what the surgeon plans to do. Only the surgeon knows.

In like-manner, only the Great Physician knows how He wants to use us. Our job is to be nothing, so that Christ can be everything. Our job is to have no will (be dead to self), so that the only will being exerted is His. Our job is to let Him do whatever His heart desires with our life, without hindering. We must be demagnetized before we can be useful to Him.

Paul wrote:

> *I am crucified with Christ: nevertheless I live; yet not I, but Christ liveth in me: and the life which I now live in the flesh I live by the faith of the Son of God, who loved me, and gave himself for me.*
>
> Galatians 2:20

Let it happen in your life today.

Chapter 8

Being a Repaired Instrument

During surgery one day I was using a certain pair of scissors. Every time I would make a cut, a small piece of tissue was left uncut, and I would have to go back and make a second cut to remove the remaining tissue. This meant I had to make two cuts to accomplish the same thing I should have accomplished with one.

This was strange, and it had never happened before, so I stopped and examined my scissors to see what was the matter. I discovered that there was a tiny chip, a missing piece from the cutting edge of one of the blades. When I tried to use it, it was like a six-year-old biting an apple with his two front teeth missing. Somehow a child manages to eat the apple, but with much more difficulty than he would experience if all of his teeth were in place.

As I reflected on the problem of the chipped scissors, it became clear to me that some of us are just like that. We are still in God's hands, but we have been marred and scarred and chipped by life's blows. We are still sterile (free from sin), and God is still willing to use us, but we are not doing a very good job for Him. Does this mean that God will cast us off? Not at all!

Let's assume that you are desperately thirsty, but you need something to get water in. As you look around, you find a beautiful pitcher. It is handpainted, with pastel flowers, and you revel in its beauty. When you look inside the pitcher, however, you are repulsed by how filthy it is. It is caked with layers of putrefying matter.

Next to this pitcher you find an old metal pot that some boys had been using as a target to try out their new BB gun. It has dents all over it, and it looks absolutely terrible. When you look inside the old pot, however, you can't help but notice that it is sparkling clean.

Tell me, from which of these two vessels would you choose to drink water? It is clear that you would choose the one that is clean on the inside and would ignore the rough outward appearance. This is the same way God operates.

When the Lord sent Samuel to anoint David as the next king over Israel, He said to him:

> *Look not on his countenance, or on the height of his stature; because I have refused him* [David's older brother]: *for the* LORD *seeth not as man seeth; for the man looketh on the outward appearance, but the* LORD *looketh on the heart.* 1 Samuel 16:7

When you look at yourself, refuse to see the limitations and to think that God cannot or will not use you. He can use any instrument that is available and sterile — even if it has a few nicks or a marred appearance. He can repair it and make it work like new again — even though it doesn't look the best.

I have instruments that I have used continually over a period of twenty-five years. The surface of these older, more used instruments may not have the brilliance of a brand new instrument, but I love them because they are tried and true and have given me a lifetime of service. I have carried them with me to China many times to do surgery and have brought them back home again. If they need to be sharpened or repaired, we have it done, and we keep right on using them.

Sometimes my instruments have gotten a little rusty from their travels. When this happens, we don't cast them away. We just use a little rust remover on them and make them shine again, and they go on doing their job.

You, too, can be used! Stop looking at your own limitations and start looking at the One who has you in His hand. He has some rust remover. He can even touch you with His healing virtue and get the chips and dents out of you. He can make your heart new again, taking away all the griefs of life, while, at the same time, retaining the unique veteran attributes.

An old friend comes to mind. Gertrude Ticer suffered from a very severe case of multiple sclerosis. She was bedridden and could not walk, she was almost blind, and at times she would have to be rushed to the hospital, when it seemed that life was ebbing out of her. Time and time again, however, as the ambulance attendants came for her, she would say to them, "Don't forget my shoes!" They thought she was crazy because they knew she had not walked in years. What did she need shoes for?

In her heart, Gertrude believed that God was going to heal her and that she would need her shoes. The Lord had been dealing with her, telling her He wanted her to preach.

She would argue back, "But Lord, I don't know the Bible very well."

"I will teach you that," He would say.

"But Lord, I am not educated," she protested.

"That doesn't matter," He would say.

"But Lord, I'm a woman."

"I noticed that," He would say.

"Lord, just heal me, and I will work at two jobs or even three jobs and give all my money to some men to preach Your Word," she offered.

"I am calling YOU to preach," He would say.

Gertrude's condition grew worse and worse, until one day she was again rushed to the hospital, this time hanging on to life by a thread. In her hospital bed, Gertrude sensed that life was leaving her body and that this might be her last chance to respond to the Lord's call. "All right, Lord," she said, "I will do as You say. I will preach."

Her body was so lifeless that the doctor could find no vital signs, so the sheet was pulled up over her head and her family was notified that she was gone.

All the hospital staff had left the room, and her cold body was alone. At that moment, in walked Jesus, the King of Kings and the Lord of Lords. He walked straight to the side of Gertrude's bed, reached over the bed rail and placed His hand on her still body. In that moment, life flooded into her with such energy that she jumped over the bed rail, ran out the door and down the hall. The nurse who had been taking care of her took one look at her and ran off screaming: "It's a ghost! It's a ghost!"

No one could believe what they were seeing. Gertrude had never walked as long as any of the hospital staff could remember her from her multiple visits. Now, suddenly, she needed her shoes. What a miracle God had done!

They kept Gertrude in the hospital for three days and did a whole series of tests on her, and every test showed that she was completely normal. During those three days, she walked up and down the halls of the hospital, and many other sick people were healed because of the faith her story inspired and the anointing God put on her life.

The thing I want you to see in all this is that it did not matter to God that Gertrude Ticer was a woman, poorly educated, unable to speak well, lacking Bible training, paralyzed, blind or even DEAD. He was able to overcome her every lack, her every inadequacy. All He wanted was A YIELDED VESSEL. It did not matter what the vessel looked like or what it had been through. He is not looking for ability; He is looking for availability.

You are surely in better shape than Gertrude Ticer was. She was dead when the Lord of Glory picked her up in His powerful hand and began using her. So stop focusing on your chips and dings and inadequacies. Focus on the Great Physician and yield your life, just as it is right now, into His mighty hand. He will use you!

Chapter 9

Being Held by an Unseen Hand

Often I do surgery on closed-circuit television. All modern eye surgery is done through an operating microscope, and when a camera is mounted on the microscope, the picture can be seen on a TV monitor in the surgery suite (for staff members to view), or in the waiting area (for the family to watch). When someone views eye surgery in this way, all they can see are the eye and the instruments

The 0.12 mm toothed forceps in the surgeon's hand

used to operate on it. They never see the hands holding the instruments because of the high magnification.

An eye is far too small and far too delicate to perform surgery on without using microsurgical instruments. But if someone viewing the procedure did not know better, they might come to the conclusion that the instruments were doing the surgery by themselves, since no human hand can be seen holding the instruments.

Looking at the TV monitor, you might see different kinds of forceps, some smooth and some with teeth, some rounded and some pointed. You might see an ultrasound instrument used to remove the cataract, as it does its job precisely. You might see various sizes and shapes of knives, each of them used for a specific task. Some of them are made of metal and some of diamond. You might see a variety of scissors, needle holders and needles. The parade of instruments goes on and on throughout the course of the surgery, and when each instrument has performed its task in conjunction with the others, the result is that an eye that was blind can now see.

Would we say of those instruments: "How smart they are! How skilled they are! How well they do their assigned task!" I think not. The truth is that mere instruments can do nothing on their own. They just happen to be what we can see. There must be a skilled surgeon holding the instruments, or they could not accomplish the task. Jesus said:

> *I am the vine, ye are the branches: He that abideth in me and I in him, the same bringeth forth much fruit: for WITHOUT ME YE CAN DO NOTHING.* John 15:5

We are just like those instruments. We can do nothing unless the Great Physician picks us up and uses us. Just because we are the ones being seen by the world does not mean we are the ones doing the work. We have no supernatural abilities of our own. We cannot make blind eyes see or crippled legs walk. When God chooses to use us as instruments to accomplish these miracles, therefore, all praise and glory must go to Him. He is the one doing the work.

We must make sure that the world around us (the viewers, if you will) understand this truth. All they see are the instruments on the screen of life doing the mending and healing, so we must make sure that they look, not to the instruments, but to the Great Physician who is holding the instruments.

I have never once had a patient come to me and say, "Please, could I see your instruments? I want to thank them for the good job they did on my eye." Never! Patients always thank the physician who holds the instruments. In the same way, we must always pass the praise on to the One really doing the work — Jesus.

I once had a lady working for me whose husband, John, was very nearsighted. Despite the fact that I was doing surgery on literally thousands of people, ridding them of their nearsightedness, John never inquired about the surgery for himself. Other employees and their spouses had the surgery, but John never seemed interested.

Then one day, after several years had passed, John came in as a patient, and, much to my surprise, said he wanted surgery to get rid of his nearsightedness. I asked him why he had not asked for the surgery much earlier. He explained that he had had a recurring nightmare since childhood in which he was having eye surgery, and he went blind. Consequently, he was very frightened by the thought of the surgery and would never pursue it.

A few nights before his visit to me, he had another dream. In this dream, he saw himself as the patient on the table, having eye surgery, with me as the surgeon. He saw Jesus come over and put His hands on top of my hands and do the operation. When the surgical procedure was finished, Jesus went to the corner of the room. This totally changed John's thinking about the surgery. Now he was no longer afraid. He was, in fact, enthusiastic about having the procedure done as soon as possible.

John had the surgery, with an excellent result, and we were all glad that God had led him to that day with a dream. Needless to say, his experience changed my thinking about surgery too and emphasized to me that it is really Jesus doing the surgery. My role is only as a yielded instrument in His hand.

We must remember what Miss Kuhlman said: "There is really no limit to what God can do with a person, providing that one will not touch the glory." If the instrument ever starts accepting praise for the works (i.e., touching the glory), he will soon be removed from the scene. God will not share His glory with anyone.

King Herod learned this lesson the hard way:

> *And upon a set day Herod, arrayed in royal apparel, sat upon his throne, and made an oration unto them. And the people gave a shout, saying, It is the voice of a god, and not of a man. And immediately the angel of the Lord smote him, because HE GAVE NOT GOD THE GLORY: and he was eaten of worms, and gave up the ghost.*   Acts 12:21-23

Even Jesus refused to touch the glory. He would always point to His Father as the Source of the words and the works. The Father was holding Jesus as an instrument in His hand:

> *Verily, verily, I say unto you, THE SON CAN DO NOTHING OF HIMSELF, but what he seeth the Father do.*   John 5:19

> *I CAN OF MINE OWN SELF DO NOTHING: as I hear, I judge.*
>   John 5:30

> *I DO NOTHING OF MYSELF; but as my Father hath taught me, I speak these things.*   John 8:28

The words that I speak unto you I SPEAK NOT OF MYSELF: but the Father that dwelleth in me, he doeth the works.

John 14:10

Just as God the Father, through the Holy Spirit, was the unseen Surgeon, doing the works in the life of Jesus, so He is still doing His works today through the Holy Spirit in us. We are the instruments seen by man, and we must continually give glory to the unseen God that holds us in His hand. Jesus said:

Verily, verily, I say unto you, He that believeth on me, the works that I do shall he do also; and greater works than these shall he do; because I go unto the Father.　　　　　John 14:12

The same Holy Spirit that worked through Jesus is working through us today, doing the works of the Father. We are a different set of instruments, created for a different day and time, but the unseen hands that hold us and use us with precision are the same.

Chapter 10

A Beloved Instrument

I have a picture frame in one of my examining rooms that displays my letter to Miss Kuhlman, her letter to me, and a picture of her on the stage in a great conference in Jerusalem. Very often patients read those letters while waiting for me to come and examine them. One day, when I walked into that room, a patient commented to me that loving an instrument was a new concept to him. He was referring to my words about the 0.12 mm toothed forceps: "I love this precision instrument."

My letter to Kathryn Kuhlman, her picture on stage in Jerusalem, and her letter to me.

This may seem strange to some, but when you rely so much on having precision instruments, you truly appreciate it when they function flawlessly. I suppose it may be necessary for most of us to have the experience of using an instrument that does not function well in order to appreciate one that does.

Once I had a forcep that was not aligned properly. Every time I would try to grasp a small piece of tissue, one jaw would slide past the other jaw. The two sides did not approximate correctly, and I could, therefore, not grasp the tissue.

This was extremely frustrating, especially if it happened at a critical time in the surgery, when there was no margin for error and no time for delay. At those moments, a surgeon must grasp the tissue quickly and precisely, and yet they cannot do it if their instrument is not working as it should. Needless to say, that broken instrument was sent away to be repaired immediately.

On another occasion, one of three teeth on an important forcep was broken off. There are two teeth on one tip of the forcep and one tooth on the other tip. The one on the one side fits between the two on the other side, and that causes the instrument to grasp wonderfully. Because one of the paired teeth was broken off, the instrument worked very poorly. It could still grasp, but with difficulty. It was not at all reliable for the type of work I do, so this instrument also was immediately sent off to be repaired.

When someone called from the repair shop to say that they could not make another tooth for the forcep, all they could do was remove the two remaining teeth and make it into a smooth forcep, I agreed to have this done. It was no longer the same instrument and would no longer serve to bite and hold tissue, but I could use it for a different purpose. This forcep was now used to tie sutures, where I needed smooth tips.

Against this backdrop of broken and poorly-functioning instruments, perhaps you can better understand how I could love an instrument that worked perfectly every time, over and over for many years. It never failed me. It always grasped tissue precisely. It was a joy to have this instrument in my hand. In fact, it felt so natural there that it became an extension of myself.

This teaches us several important things about being God's people. We are instruments in His hand, and, like me, He loves to have an instrument that will accomplish His purposes precisely. Sometimes a person may get out of alignment like the forcep that would not approximate correctly, but how wonderful it is to know that God can put us into His repair shop and fix us — if we allow Him to do it! It matters not if the malady that affects us be of the heart, the mind or the body. He can fix it — whatever it is — and put us back into service.

There is no question that some things in the natural are unfixable, but with God nothing is impossible. Sometimes people try so hard to fix themselves or ask others to try and fix them, but, in reality, the only one who can really do this repair job is Jesus.

Sometimes I go to retirement homes or nursing homes and visit those who are in the latter years of their lives. They have been so active and "on the go" all their lives, and now they are forced to lean on a walker or sit in a wheelchair to get around. For those of you who fit this description, I want to remind you of the forcep that had its function changed. It no longer had teeth, but it was still very useful in my hands. Perhaps God blessed you to teach Sunday school, sing in the choir or even preach the Gospel, and you no longer have the ability to do these things. Don't think for a single minute, however, that you are less useful to God than you used to be. You can still spread light wherever you are. You can still be an intercessor and touch nations and influence circumstances. Remember the Lord's promise:

The effectual fervent prayer of a righteous man availeth much.
James 5:16

You can be just as useful to God or even more useful to Him in your prayer closet than you were when you were more mobile. Perhaps your function has changed, from a running warrior to a praying warrior, but as long as you are still in His hand, He will use you. Paul wrote to the Philippians:

> *It is God which worketh in you both to will and to do of his good pleasure.*   Philippians 2:13

My pastor often told the story of an evangelist who went to hold meetings in a certain church. The pastor of the church asked the evangelist to accompany him on a visit to the family of an elderly man who had been a faithful member of the church, but who had just died. On the way to the man's home, the pastor commented that the man who had just died had been a quiet man who never said much and was not known to have contributed much to the life of the church.

While the pastor was visiting with the family, the evangelist wandered through the house by himself. It was a small house and humble. As he walked into the bedroom, the Lord spoke to him to look on the back side of the dead man's bed, between the bed and the wall. When he looked there, he saw imprints worn into the floor, where the man had knelt for hours, praying, day in and day out, year in and year out. The Spirit spoke to the evangelist, telling him that this man's prayers had been the sole supporting factor in that church, and that the church would fall now that its prayer support was gone.

The evangelist said nothing about this at the time, but hid it in his heart. A few years later, he came through that same town and inquired about the church. "Oh, it was closed down," was the response. The evangelist knew why. When that praying man died, so did the church. He had carried it through his prayers. Although he had not been recognized by others as making a significant contribution, his had been the most important support of all.

I tell this story to emphasize the power and importance of prayer. Never underestimate how vitally important you are as an intercessor. When lives are changed and souls are won to Christ, it is because of a partnership between the person going and the person praying to undergird him or her.

If your function has changed as an instrument, don't be sad that you no longer do what you used to do, but rather rejoice that you are still a useful, functional instrument in the hand of the Great Physician. However He chooses to use you is perfect in His sight. You, too, can be a reliable, precision instrument year after year. You, too, can be an instrument BELOVED of the Lord.

Chapter 11

Being Controlled by the Holy Spirit

Some might ask if the Holy Spirit is critical to being an instrument in God's hand. The answer is emphatically yes. When we look back to the life of Jesus, we can see this clearly.

Undoubtedly Jesus was a wonderful boy growing up. When He was only twelve years old, He remained behind in the Temple in Jerusalem, and when His parents came looking for Him, He said to them: *"Didn't you know that I must be about My Father's business?"* (Luke 2:49, my paraphrase). Instead of being focused on playing games, like most twelve-year-old boys, Jesus was focused on learning the Word of God and doing His Father's business.

We know that Jesus was *"without sin,"* so we know He did no wrong. In fact the day He went down into the Jordan River and was baptized by John the Baptist, the Father spoke from Heaven and said:

Thou art my beloved Son; in thee I am well pleased. Luke 3:22

During the first thirty years of the life of Jesus, He was a kind, gentle, wonderful, sinless man. Still, He did no miracles. Why? Because He lacked the power of the Holy Spirit. This came to him the day he was baptized in the Jordan River, when the Holy Spirit descended on Him like a dove. After that day, the Word of God clearly shows us, it was the Holy Spirit who was filling Jesus and leading Him and empowering Him and anointing Him to do the works of God:

And Jesus being FULL OF THE HOLY GHOST returned from Jordan, and was LED BY THE SPIRIT into the wilderness.

Luke 4:1

And Jesus returned IN THE POWER OF THE SPIRIT into Galilee: and there went out a fame of him through all the region round about. Luke 4:14

How God ANOINTED JESUS OF NAZARETH WITH THE HOLY GHOST and with power: who went about doing good, and healing all that were oppressed of the devil; for God was with him. Acts 10:38

Clearly then, the Holy Spirit was the source of power in the man, Jesus. From the day when the Holy Spirit descended on Him, Jesus changed water into wine, He healed sick bodies, He spoke the words of life, He fed multitudes with a boy's small lunch, and He made devils flee. In a word, He did the works of God through the power of the Holy Spirit. He stated this very clearly Himself:

But if I cast out devils BY THE SPIRIT OF GOD, then the kingdom of God is come unto you. Matthew 12:28

If the power of the Holy Spirit was critical to Jesus being an instrument for the miraculous in the hand of God, how much more so in the life of His followers. Jesus commanded His disciples to stay in Jerusalem and *"wait for the promise of the Father,"* which was to *"be baptized with the Holy Ghost"* (Acts 1:4-5). He explained the purpose of the baptism in the Holy Spirit this way:

But ye shall RECEIVE POWER, after that the Holy Ghost is come upon you: and ye shall BE WITNESSES UNTO ME both in

Jerusalem, and in all Judaea, and in Samaria, and unto the uttermost part of the earth.   Acts 1:8

To me, Peter is a perfect example of what a person is like, with and without the baptism in the Holy Spirit. On the night Jesus was betrayed He said to His disciples:

You will all be offended and stumble and fall away because of Me this night.   Matthew 26:31, Amplified

Peter was sure it would never happen to him:

Peter declared to Him, though they all are offended and stumble and fall away because of You and distrust and desert You, I will never do so.
Jesus said to him, Solemnly I declare to you, this very night before a single rooster crows you will deny and disown Me three times.
Peter said to Him, Even if I must die with You, I will not deny or disown You! And all the disciples said the same thing.
      Matthew 26:33-35, Amplified

Peter was adamant. He would NEVER leave Jesus — even if they killed him — and he surely believed this with every fiber of his being. He was certain that NOTHING could ever make him turn his back on his Master.

When they arrested Jesus, Peter was brave enough to follow Him at a distance, but when recognized as having been with Jesus, he denied it vigorously. He made this denial not just once, but three times, the third time with cursing and swearing.

He had tried his best to be brave and stand by his Lord, but when faced with persecution and possible execution himself, Peter's flesh was simply not strong enough to stand up, even to a young maiden who was one of those who accused him. The arm of flesh was too weak. He could not even admit he knew Jesus, much less be a witness that He was the Messiah, the King of Kings and Lord of Lords.

Fifty days later, on the Day of Pentecost, one hundred and twenty believers — including Peter — were waiting together, as Jesus had instructed them, when something wonderful happened:

> *And suddenly there came a sound from heaven as of a rushing mighty wind and it filled all the house where they were sitting. And there appeared unto them cloven tongues like as of fire, and it sat upon each of them. And they were all filled with the Holy Ghost, and began to speak with other tongues, as the Spirit gave them utterance.* Acts 2:2-4

Peter was still the same man. He had the same hair and teeth and bones. His face had not changed. He was not any taller or stronger than he had been just a month and a half before when he had denied Christ three times. Now, however, he had received the promise of the Father, the baptism with the Holy Spirit, the power to be a witness. He no longer was acting or speaking in his own human power; rather, the powerful Holy Spirit was acting and speaking through him.

Peter stood up in the middle of the huge crowd that had gathered, looked into the faces of the same men who had shouted, "Crucify Him, Crucify Him," causing Jesus to be tortured and hung on a cross. He was no longer afraid because he was no longer operating in his own limited strength. He was able to speak boldly by the power of the Holy Spirit, saying:

> *Jesus of Nazareth, a man approved of God among you by miracles and wonders and signs, which God did by him in the midst of you, as ye yourselves also know: ... ye have taken, and by wicked*

hands have crucified and slain: ... Repent, and be baptized every one of you in the name of Jesus Christ for the remission of sins, and ye shall receive the gift of the Holy Ghost.

Acts 2:22-23 and 38

Peter's sermon that day was so powerful, so moving, that three thousand souls were saved and baptized. How could a man be so radically changed from someone cowering before a young girl to a man speaking without fear to thousands? There is only one explanation: the baptism in the Holy Spirit.

The Spirit was speaking through Peter now, and it was exactly as Jesus had foretold:

Ye shall receive POWER, after that the HOLY GHOST is come upon you, and ye shall be WITNESSES unto me.　　Acts 1:8

Jesus has not changed, and He is saying the same thing to us today. He wants to give us the same gift of the baptism in the Holy Spirit that He gave the one hundred and twenty on the Day of Pentecost, and for the same purpose — so that we might be His witnesses, so that we might be instruments in His hand.

Chapter 12

Being the Great Physician's Instrument

I was shocked one day when I went in for a routine physical examination and was told that there was a suspicious mass in my abdomen that needed to be removed as soon as possible. I had been feeling well, with no symptoms of anything amiss whatsoever, so this news took me quite by surprise. After getting a second opinion, I agreed to proceed with the surgery right away. As I prayed about it, the Lord assured me that everything would turn out fine. He said to me, "Your body will preach to them." I had no idea what this meant, but I had learned a long time ago to accept whatever God said — whether I understood it or not.

When the day arrived, a small group of friends were gathered in the hospital room with me as I waited to be taken to surgery. We had been singing songs unto the Lord for about fifteen minutes, when someone began singing:

We are standing on holy ground
And I know that there are angels all around … .

Suddenly I heard an announcement in the Spirit: "The Great Physician is here." Simultaneously, I saw Jesus standing at the foot of my bed, with what looked like four large men (they must have been angels) standing beside Him and behind Him.

This proclamation, "The Great Physician ... ," had a huge impact on me. Here I was in a large medical center with hundreds of doctors around. Some of them were probably viewed as great physicians. I was a doctor too, but all this faded into insignificance in the presence of the One and Only Great Physician, Jesus. There was no other "great physician" but Him.

It reminded me of the time when the rich young ruler had a conversation with Jesus:

> *Behold, one came and said unto him, Good Master, what good thing shall I do, that I may have eternal life? And he said unto him, Why callest thou me good? there is none good but one, that is, God ... .* Matthew 19:16-17

In much the same way, I have felt since the day God spoke to me in the hospital that there is no great physician except the Great Physician, Jesus.

Just after I saw Him, a nurse entered the room and rolled my bed into surgery, and I saw my Great Physician follow along behind the bed with his honor guard of angels.

Obviously, there is nothing to fear when Jesus is there to be your surgeon, your anesthesiologist, your nurse — your everything. Since that day, it is easy for me to pray and believe God for other people facing surgery. He is *"no respecter of persons."* If He will go with me into surgery, He will go with anyone who will ask Him.

The surgery was done late on a Thursday afternoon, and I do not remember much about Thursday night. Friday morning, however, when I woke up, I was determined to aid in my own speedy recovery. The surgeon had told me that the more I would exercise, the faster I would recover, so I proceeded to get out of bed that morning and walk laps around the ward where I was staying. I had a large incision all the way down my abdomen, but I forced myself to walk anyway.

Every time someone came to visit me that day, I would walk a few more laps with them. By nightfall of my first day after surgery, I had walked four miles — a record for that hospital. My surgeon began telling this story to every patient facing surgery so they would be encouraged to exercise as much and as soon as possible.

I recovered so quickly that I missed only six days from my office, despite that fact that it had been considered "major surgery," and I was back doing surgery myself in less than two weeks. I guess that astounding recovery is what God meant when He said, "Your body will preach to them." I am sure that this quick recovery was a result of the perfect love and care given to me by the Great Physician, not just my willingness to exercise.

The thing that surprised me was not that the Lord was with me in surgery, for I knew He would be. It was that He allowed me to see Him in the Spirit, thus making it an even more vivid reality to me (and I hope to you). It showed me again that God cares a great deal about the health of our physical bodies. He said:

> *I am the LORD that HEALETH thee.*   *Exodus 15:26*

> *Beloved, I wish above all things that thou mayest prosper and be in HEALTH, even as thy soul prospereth.*   3 John 2

Our God cares so much about each of us that He sent His only Son, Jesus, to sacrifice His body so that our bodies might be healed:

> *Surely our griefs* [SICKNESS] *He Himself bore, and our sorrows* [PAINS] *He carried;*
> *Yet we ourselves esteemed Him stricken, smitten of God and afflicted.*
> *But He was pierced through [wounded] for our transgressions,*
> *He was crushed for our iniquities;*

The chastening for our well-being [peace] *fell upon Him, and by His scourging we are HEALED.*   Isaiah 53:4-5 NAS

... by whose stripes ye were HEALED.   1 Peter 2:24

In other words, Christ took a beating so severe that it brought Him near death, too weak to carry His cross, and all because He wanted us to have health in our bodies. How wonderful!

The Roman soldiers commonly used a whip with several thongs. At the end of each of those thongs was tied a piece of sharp, weighted metal or bone that was capable of tearing the flesh each time the whip was used. When they finished the "stripes" or "scourging" or beating, therefore, it left Jesus near death with blood loss and in extreme agony, with the muscles in His back torn to shreds and probably bone or entrails exposed.

Jesus did not have to take this beating. He could have called on angels to deliver Him, but He did it for us, so that we could be healed.

Some people feel that God's healing is not for today. I think these scriptures clearly disprove that theory.

Some people go to the other extreme, feeling that we should not go to a doctor or take medicine at all, but only trust in God to heal us. I had an experience not long ago that sheds light on this matter.

A pastor's wife came to me wanting laser surgery to correct her severe nearsightedness. I did a thorough examination and felt she was a good candidate for the surgery, so a date was set for the operation. Just as we were going to take her to surgery, she asked if she could tell me of an experience she had the night before. She said she awoke at 4:30 a.m., full of fear about the eye surgery and prayed: "Lord, I can't do this."

The Lord spoke to her and said, "I want to perform a miracle for you, and I want to do it through Dr. Elizabeth Vaughan's hands." He reminded her of her childhood, when she had strong faith and would believe God for anything. Time after time, she would put her hands over her eyes and ask God to do a miracle to rid her of her severe nearsightedness. Each time she would believe that when she removed her hands she would be able to see, but the miracle never happened.

By the time she was a teenager, she finally accepted the reality that she could not see without thick glasses or contact lenses, so she stopped praying about it. Now, twenty to twenty-five years had passed, and she had long-ago forgotten about asking God for a miracle of vision. But the Lord said, "I didn't forget. I heard every one of those prayers, and I want to answer those prayers for you."

After hearing from God and knowing that He would do a miracle for her, great peace flooded her being, where fear had been. She was calm and quiet, with a smile on her face, as we led her into surgery. The next day she was seeing very well without glasses for the first time she could ever remember in her life. We both thanked God and rejoiced greatly.

It is not easy to explain just how much the words God spoke to this lady have meant to me as a surgeon. We tend to think of medical and surgical treatment as a natural phenomenon, but God said He was going to do a MIRACLE through the hands of a surgeon, and if God says something, we are compelled to believe it — whether we understand all of its ramifications or not. I gave my medical practice to God when I gave my life to Him in 1973. I had always viewed it as the practice of medicine, but God had declared that He was in the practice of miracles through the practice of medicine.

We must understand from this that God is God, and He can heal any way He wants, either with or without medical (or surgical) intervention. It is a miracle when God heals through prayer alone, but it is also a miracle when He heals through medicine or surgery.

Either way, He is the one who deserves the glory, for He is the Great Physician.

When I clean my kitchen at home, I use some yellow rubber gloves. As I handle dishes or wipe the counter tops, it is not the gloves doing these functions, it is my hands in the gloves doing the work. That is easy for us to understand. What has not been as easy for us to understand is that when we have consecrated our lives to the Lord, then He is living in us just like the hand is in the glove.

Paul wrote:

> ... *Christ IN YOU, the hope of glory.*   Colossians 1:27

If the Lord is in control of your life, if He is the Lord of your life, then He can do whatever He wants through you. It stands to reason, then, that He can indeed do surgery through a surgeon's hands, as He told my patient. He can also love through your heart or speak through your mouth or hug through your arms. Actually He can do anything through us that we will allow Him to do. All He needs is our yieldedness.

Allow the Great Physician to use you today and do surgery on the hearts and minds and souls of the people around you. Whether you are a surgeon, a housewife, a businessman ... whatever work fills your days, never forget that you are an instrument in God's hand.

Part III:

Reaching Out to the World

Chapter 13

The Jerusalem Connection
and My First Trips to China

In November of 1979, I was visiting Jerusalem with a friend named Geri. We had both been there before, so we decided to venture into a part of the Old City where neither of us had ever been. We had strolled through the streets for quite a while when suddenly we realized that we were in a very different part of the city. There were

With Geri, at the Damascus Gate in Jerusalem.

With Ruth, Geri, and friend, in a Jerusalem restaurant.

private walls everywhere we turned. It was like a maze of walls with periodic locked gates. There were no people around, no shops anywhere. We were lost. We tried to find our way back to the busy section of the city, but everywhere we turned more silent walls presented themselves.

By this time the sun was going down, and we were beginning to get a bit concerned that we might have to spend the night in the street, leaning against a wall. We started asking the Lord to help us find our way out of the maze of narrow streets.

As we prayed we kept walking in the growing dusk, until we finally saw an elderly man approaching. He had something rolled up in a newspaper under his arm. We had no idea if he spoke English or not, but we were compelled to try to communicate with him. We asked him what part of the city we were in.

Thank God the gentleman understood the question and told us

that we were in the Armenian section. Geri, being a very gregarious person, asked him if he knew Demos Shakarian, the founder of the Full Gospel Businessmen's Fellowship, the only Armenian she knew. To our amazement, he said he did know of Mr. Shakarian. This opened the door for him to tell us that he was a Christian, and he proceeded to invite us to come to his home and meet his wife.

We followed this man to a small, humble home, where his wife demonstrated the local hospitality by proceeding to serve us rolled oats with cinnamon and a little sugar.

The most prized possession in the little house was an old upright piano, which neither of them played. It was carefully covered with a nice cloth. When they learned that Geri was a pianist, they asked her to play for them. Glory rolled out of that old piano as she played, and tears came to their eyes at the joy of having music in their home for the first time in many years. God blessed them and blessed us through that meeting within the maze of walls in the Old Armenian Quarter of Jerusalem.

Before we left his house that night this gentleman told us of a meeting being held in the church known as St. Peter-en-Gallicantu by an American lady from Virginia. He invited us to go there the following Friday night, and we said we would. We had no idea that we were about to begin a whole new chapter of our lives.

When we arrived at the church that Friday night, promptly at 7:00 p.m., many people were already there, and they were dancing in front of the altar and singing joyfully. Not one person was sitting back in the pews. We had never been in a church service like this, and we really did not know what to do. We just stood quietly in one of the pews, watching what was happening.

Before long, one of the believers came over to us and invited us to join the group, so we went to the front and started dancing with the others. They were doing line dancing and circle dancing, and they were singing what we later learned to be the "new song." Some-

Walking where Jesus walked. The Roman road leading to the place
where our Lord was mocked and beaten.

one in the group would receive a song spontaneously from the Lord
and begin to sing it. These "new songs" were always simple enough
that we could all catch on to them quickly and sing together.

Then another person would get a second verse to the same song
or perhaps they would get another "new song" from the Lord, and
again everyone would join in. This spontaneous singing and dancing went on for a full hour, with no apparent leader except the Holy
Spirit.

As everyone began to sit down, a tall lady came over to me and
said, "Haven't we met before?"

I had never seen her before in my life, so I told her no, we hadn't.

She looked at me intently and said, "I'm sure we have met before."

Again I told her we had never met.

Persistent in her belief that we had met, she looked at my face carefully and then said, "I remember! I saw you on the Phil Donohue Show when I was in America." Sure enough, I had been on the Phil Donohue Show with Rev. R.W. Schambach, verifying a miracle God had done on a man who had lost his eye. That she had remembered a stranger's face from a single television show was a great miracle, but I was to learn that this woman was surrounded by the miraculous.

She introduced herself as Ruth Heflin, head of the Mt. Zion Fellowship, based in Jerusalem. She asked me if I would speak at their church on Mt. Zion the next day, which was the Sabbath. Still in a stunned state because of this series of strange events, I accepted the invitation. It was the beginning of a lifelong friendship with Ruth.

The next morning the Lord told me to speak about "walking on the water" (i.e., walking by faith), which I had had abundant practice in doing over the preceding years. Immediately after the service, Ruth graciously thanked me for coming and then scurried away to take care of some important business. Months later I learned just what that important business was.

The fellowship had a team of people ready to go into China. They had been waiting in Hong Kong and Los Angeles for several months, unable to get visas. They were running out of funds, and Ruth needed to make an immediate decision about whether or not to bring them home. She had prayed fervently, asking God to give her a definite word through me that Sabbath morning about what to do concerning China. The strong word that had come forth was "walk on the water," so she acted immediately on this word and bought herself a ticket to fly to Hong Kong via Los Angeles on the next flight leaving Israel. In faith, she was believing that God would open the door for the team to enter China.

The Lord had told Ruth, "On Thanksgiving Day, you will have

something to be thankful for." Thanksgiving had only been a few days away when I spoke at the Mt. Zion Fellowship. Ruth arrived in Hong Kong on Thanksgiving Day. Her team met her with the news that, after waiting all those months, they had just gotten their Chinese visas. God's timing is perfect, and His ways are awesome to behold! The team members had a wonderful Thanksgiving together in Hong Kong, before entering China.

Falling in Love

Not knowing anything about this situation with China, I was on my way home from Israel when the Lord spoke to me and said, "Go to China, and do it now." I had been away from my practice for several weeks already, and this meant that my desk would be stacked high with paper work and my patient load would be unusually heavy on my return. It did not seem like a good time to take another trip, but I could not consider the circumstances. Nothing else mattered at the moment except obeying God.

As soon as I got back home, I went to work trying to get a visa into China. I tried and tried, but I could not seem to get a visa. Finally, I decided that I would just go on to Hong Kong and work on getting a visa there. If God had said for me to go to China now, He would surely make a way for me to get in. So I set off in the dead of winter for my first experience with China.

When I arrived in Hong Kong, I went immediately to the visa office and applied for a visa to the Mainland. After considerable effort, I was assigned to a group of eight English-speaking tourists with a tour guide, and was at last given the necessary visa. I was on my way.

Our guide took us across the southern Chinese border to Canton (now called Guangzhou) where the weather in January was similar to our Miami in winter. We wore light jackets and walked about in the markets with the sun shining brightly on us. It was delightful.

The Chinese were all dressed in Mao jackets and pants, mostly in navy blue or gray, men and women alike. Everyone that was not walking was on a bicycle, as there were very few motorized vehicles. I had never seen so many people and so many bicycles in my life! After all, about one-quarter of the world's population lives in China.

From this mild weather in the south, we flew to Beijing, which is more like Minnesota in the winter. The temperature was below freezing, and we were taken directly from the airport on a walking tour of the Forbidden City, with no opportunity to get out some heavier clothing from our luggage, which had been taken to the hotel in a separate vehicle.

The Forbidden City is like a walled city within a city where former emperors lived and from which they ruled. Their former mansions are now open to the public, replete with grand furnishings and displays of the silk embroidered gowns they wore. It is a place where anyone would be happy to spend many hours, and we did so that day, even in our frozen state.

Meals were served to us on a round, moveable platform in the center of the table, similar to our "lazy susans." Each person had chopsticks to eat with. The same chopsticks were used to serve oneself from the center dishes, since no serving utensils were provided. After walking all day in the cold, many of our group got sick. This was compounded by the fact that there was no heat in the hotels or in any other public buildings. Since we all had to use our personal chopsticks to serve ourselves, we shared each other's illnesses as well as the food. We were sick with a variety of upper respiratory and gastrointestinal ailments.

Some might be wondering how anyone could love such a place. The answer is simple: the Chinese people. Never in America or in any of my travels to other parts of the world had I ever seen such honesty and such childlike simplicity. There were no locks on the hotel doors. You could leave your gold jewelry or a stack of hundred-dollar bills on the table and not worry about it being stolen. The maids would pick it up, dust under it and carefully place it back where it had been.

Even though we did not speak the same language and could not communicate, you could sense the sweet humility of the people and their desire to make our stay a pleasant one.

Simple pleasures, like a little bird in a cage or a cup of very hot tea, would make these people happy and satisfy them. They did not need shopping malls with neon lights and three hundred kinds of athletic shoes to stimulate them and make them happy, as seems to be the case with some of us Westerners these days. They did not know such things existed. They were happy with a bowl of rice, a few vegetables, and being able to share these things with their families and friends. There were smiles all around.

Though possessions were meager among the Chinese people, their hearts seemed to overflow. I came to love the Chinese people more than I can describe. It seemed like God had put a piece of His heart inside of me and filled me with love for the Chinese people.

During the cultural revolution many of them had been imprisoned and many died, but the indomitable spirit of the Chinese people lived on. I have a Chinese woman working for me in Dallas, and when something difficult arises, she says, "I am Chinese, I can bear it." It is an attitude that no matter what hardships are imposed on me, I will endure; I can take it; I will not crumble — and so the Chinese culture has been for thousands of years. Surely God must have had China in His hand, holding her up by His grace, for her to have survived so long through so much.

On that first trip, we were taken to the Great Wall of China. What an awesome structure! It was built over a period of several hundred years, beginning more than two thousand, two hundred years ago, and took the lives of many men in the process. It is about four thousand miles long, so long and so large that the Apollo II astronauts said it was the only man-made structure visible from space.

As I climbed the steep steps to the wall and walked so far on it that no one else was around, the Spirit of the Lord came upon me to prophesy to that great nation. I stood facing south, overlooking most of China, and spoke the words of God out loud to the wind. I stated that there would be waves and waves of the Spirit that would sweep across the land, preparing her for the coming of Christ. I took a small rock from the Great Wall that day, and I still have it to remind me of that important moment in time.

It was still freezing cold in Beijing, and the full-length wool coat I had taken with me from Dallas was no match for the icy wind that cut through it as if it were made of chiffon. One day I went to a local department store in Beijing to look for something warmer to wear. I was the only blond, blue-eyed person most of the Chinese people had ever seen, and they would gather around me on the streets and just stare, like I had come from another planet. They

On the Great Wall of China, wearing the famous red silk jacket, January 1980.

would speak excitedly to their children and point at me, like I was a rare, near-extinct African rhino in the zoo.

As I walked into the store that day and began to try on silk jackets, I had a huge crowd watching me — almost as if I were a coat model. Modeling had never been an aspiration of mine, but unwittingly, that is what I was doing. The crowd seemed especially amused when I bought a red jacket. Later I learned that the Chinese often wore red silk when they got married.

That red jacket had layers of finely-woven silk padding in it, and the wind could not penetrate it. It was, thankfully, very warm. From the day I bought it, the only time I took it off the entire time I was in China was to sleep at night. I was wearing that red jacket when prophesying on the Great Wall, and I wore it for almost twenty years off and on after I returned to Dallas. It became my favorite jacket of all times.

The food on the trip had been less than desirable. Those of us on the tour never knew for sure what we were eating, and we certainly did not want to ask. When you are sick, you don't have much appetite anyway. Throughout the trip, however, we had been told that when we got to Wuhan we would have a wonderful banquet by a lake with a surprise delicacy. We had been looking forward to this wonderful meal in a picturesque setting for days.

Finally the day came, and we arrived in Wuhan. The lake was frozen, but we were still excited about what our special treat was to be. As we sat at the table, chop sticks in hand, waiting to attack this delicacy, a waiter brought out a big platter and set it in the middle of the table. On it was a large carp, cooked whole, with its head, eyeballs, tail and even its large scales, still attached. Over the fish had been poured a black sauce.

"How do you eat such a thing?" you might ask. Well, you take your chopsticks and grab a big bite of meat, skin, bones, scales and black sauce. They say beauty is in the eye of the beholder. I believe deliciousness is in the taste of the eater, too. To some, this special kind of fish was a delicacy they could never have afforded. To others, it was something they did not even want to look at, much less eat. Culture and tradition do make a difference — sometimes a very big difference.

I came home full. My lungs were full of pneumonia, but, far more importantly and more enduring, my heart was full of love for the Chinese people. This was a love the Spirit would blow on, making the flames grow higher with time, creating a fire which could not be quenched.

The Dream

I made my second trip to China in the fall of that same year. This time I went with a small group, including Nora Lam and the astronaut, Jim Irwin. Because we were with the famous astronaut, we were given special treatment and got to stay at the beautiful State House in Beijing where the Chinese normally house visiting dignitaries. The weather was beautiful, the people were still smiling and sweet, and I fell deeper in love with China.

It seemed odd, therefore, when I did not go back to China for many years. Then, in March of 1994, I was invited by the Chinese Academy of Medical Sciences to go to Beijing and lecture on modern eye surgery. I wondered if they would want me to perform surgery.

This brought up another important question. Should I take my own instruments in case the hospital where I would be teaching didn't have the instruments I needed? I was hesitant to take them. As I have described, my instruments for microsurgery are very delicate and expensive. If an instrument was not handled with care, it could be damaged, and it would cost me several thousand dollars to replace it.

Two friends would be accompanying me, Geri and Susan, both veterans of the mission field. I thought I might teach one of them

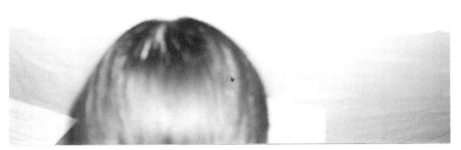

Teaching modern cataract surgery to eye surgeons in Beijing, 1994.

how to care for my instruments. Susan would have been the most likely candidate, but she was too far away, in Virginia. Geri, although she lived in Dallas, was the kind of person who has a very real aversion to all things medical. If something surgical came on the television, I had known her to leave the room. She did not want to hear about surgery, much less see it. Would I dare ask her to learn about my surgical instruments?

Because of proximity, Geri was the only logical choice, so I asked her if she would be willing to learn to care for my instruments. Much to my surprise, she immediately said she would. I could not imagine why she had so quickly and easily agreed to be involved with surgery, which she so obviously and vigorously disliked. Then she shared a dream with me that God had given her several months before. In the dream she was pushing my surgical instruments on a very old cart in a room, which she remembered vividly. The room had dark wood paneling, with hallways going out of it in several directions. She noted foreign faces on the medical personnel, but she did not know what country she was in.

This dream had made such in impression on Geri that she readily agreed to learn about the care of my surgical instruments. It is interesting how a word or a dream from God can completely change one's thinking. Geri learned a little about my instruments, and off we went with them to China.

The morning I was to lecture, we were picked up at the hotel and taken to a highly revered medical institution that had been built by John D. Rockefeller in 1921 on property originally owned by the Presbyterian Church. It was like the Harvard of China. The head of the Ophthalmology Department met us, and he and I began walking together into the building. Geri and Susan followed us a few feet behind.

As we walked into the large wood-paneled room, I heard someone say, "This is it! This is it!" I turned, and tears were streaming down Geri's face. This was the exact room God had shown her in the dream about nine months previously.

Susan said blandly, "Oh, we've traveled among the nations by vision for years." But Geri's bubble was not burst. She was overwhelmed that God would show her the inside of a hospital room on the opposite side of the world and then take her to that very spot. The Scriptures declare:

The steps of a good man are ordered by the LORD: and he delighteth in his way.   Psalm 37:23

In the years ahead, we often told this story to the Chinese people, and many of them, who were not supposed to believe in God, would say, "Surely the God has sent you to us."

I lectured that day to a room full of eye surgeons from all over Beijing about several modern techniques, including phaco-emulsification, an ultrasound technique used to remove cataracts. The doctors at the host hospital wanted to learn how to do this technique, so they made plans to buy the equipment and asked if I could come back to teach them how to use it. I agreed to return in the fall.

This was the beginning of a snowball effect in our work in China. As the old saying goes, *God works in mysterious ways His wonders to perform.* Little did we know then how He would use us as instruments in His hands in China. Already in my heart, however, there was being birthed a desire to help the poor people in that great land.

Imprisoned for Christ.

We also met many wonderful Christians in China. On one of my first trips into the country, for example, I met a Catholic priest, whom I will call Father Wu. He had an amazing story. He was very bright and very consecrated to Christ, so while he was yet a young priest, his elders selected him to be sent to the Vatican for special training. He could read, write and speak seven languages.

During Father Wu's time at the Vatican, the situation in China became very difficult, with Christians being severely persecuted. In his heart, he wanted to return to China to bring as much comfort as he could to his people, but his superiors strongly advised against his going back because it would be too dangerous for him. "My sheep need me," he said, and left for China, despite the personal danger he knew he would surely face.

When Father Wu arrived in his native land, the predictable happened. He was arrested. Instead of killing him, the authorities realized that he could be useful to them as a translator, so they put him into solitary confinement and made him translate war documents from other languages into Chinese. He was permitted no Bible and no fellowship.

Father Wu remained thus isolated in prison for twenty-five years. When I asked him how he had survived during those long and lonely years, he said that as a young Christian he had memorized the entire book of John. Though he had no access to the Bible in prison, he had it hidden in his heart, where no man could take it away. The Word of God in his heart sustained him like nothing else could have.

Jesus said:

Man shall not live by bread alone, but by every word that proceedeth out of the mouth of God.   Matthew 4:4

Ever since he was released from prison, Father Wu has been actively serving Jesus as a priest. He says that he considers it an honor to have been persecuted for the cause of Christ. There is no bitterness or sorrow in this man, only rejoicing in the life of Christ that flows through him. If you were to meet him, you would probably never guess that he had been imprisoned or had spent twenty-five years in solitary confinement. He reminds me of Shadrach, Meshach and Abednego who were thrown into a fiery furnace in the time of the prophet Daniel because of their relentless devotion to God:

> *... upon whose bodies the fire had no power, nor was an hair of their head singed, neither were their coats changed, nor the smell of fire had passed on them.*   Daniel 3:27

In other words, you could not tell by their appearance that they had been anywhere near fire. Too many Christians, when they have a little adversity, want to dwell on it and talk about it and show their scars, trying to elicit pity or to augment their own self-pity. This is not a healthy response to suffering and is, in fact, opposite to the teaching of the Word of God concerning the response God desires to see in us:

> *Consider it all joy, my brethren, when you encounter various trials, knowing that the testing of your faith produces endurance. And let endurance have its perfect result, that you may be perfect and complete, lacking in nothing.*   James 1:2-4, NAS

We must never forget the promise we cling to in adversity:

> *And we know that all things work together for good to them that love God, to them who are the called according to his purpose.*
>   Romans 8:28

So if you love God, if you are called according to His purpose, know that He will work everything out for your good and, ultimately, for His good. Remember how Shadrach, Meshach and Abednego were honored and promoted to high positions in the government, and their God was highly exalted — all because He brought them through the fire.

Father Wu holds a high position in his church today because he went through the fire victoriously with God, and you, too, can go through your fire with great triumph, if you will keep your eyes fixed on Jesus — because you trust in Him.

The people of China were stealing my heart, and I sensed that God would use us to bless them. This was confirmed in a very unusual way.

Money From Heaven

Our last stop before leaving China that first year was the southern city of Guangzhou. It had changed dramatically in fourteen years. All of China had changed dramatically. Some changes were quite noticeable. For one, the people were no longer dressed in their blue or gray Mao jackets and trousers. The large majority of them had on western-style clothes, and many wore blue jeans. Strangely enough, it was now hard to find any Chinese-style clothing for sale. I had to go to a store for tourists to find another silk jacket like the red one I had loved so much.

The streets of China were still crowded, but there were fewer bicycles and many more cars on the streets. Because Guangzhou is so close to Hong Kong, there was more western influence there than in other parts of China. Commerce was bustling, and, with their newfound freedoms, people were eager to make money.

We were walking through an open market one day in which you could find everything from pearls to snakes and live shrimp for sale. A few of the things we saw that day were not pleasant. Probably the worst for me was a cat, skinned and ready to eat. Another thing shocked me as well. As I stood beside a wall and watched as others shopped, my eyes fell on some small bundles of something I could not recognize. I stared at it for a long time, wondering what it might be. Some of the bundles were about three inches high, and others were four to five inches high. I took a few steps closer to try see them more clearly and be able to solve the mystery. Much to my surprise, I recognized that these were dried centipedes of varying lengths. People eat the strangest things in south China!

The last morning we were in China was on a Sunday. Susan had worked in China for years and developed a relationship with pastors in various parts of the country. She wanted to visit a certain Three-Self church, the current equivalent of all protestant denominations combined. There are only two types of government recognized and approved churches in China — the Catholic Church and the Three-Self Church. Both are open to whoever wants to worship there.

We went to church that Sunday morning and respectfully sat through the whole service in Chinese. Some of the hymns were recognizable because of the melodies. It is amazing that many of the same songs we sing to glorify Jesus are sung around the world. Fruit is still growing from seeds planted by missionaries in centuries past.

After the service, Susan spoke to the senior pastor, whom she knew. He took us, along with another of his associate pastors, to a room in a small building behind the church, and there the five of us sat in a semicircle visiting. The door to the room was open and, after a few minutes, a robust Chinese man walked into the room uninvited and came straight over to me. He stood in front of me and said in perfect English, "Why are you here? Why have you come to China?"

I had no idea who this man was or why he was interrupting our meeting with the pastors. Was he a government agent of some sort? I certainly had done nothing wrong and had nothing to fear. Why did he come straight to me and speak to no one else?

I simply told the man the truth. I had been invited by the Chinese

Academy of Medical Sciences to lecture in Beijing on modern eye surgery. It was in my heart to reach out to the poor people in rural China and to provide them with free eye surgery. We would be returning soon to pursue this further.

He said nothing, but reached into his back pocket and pulled out his wallet. I thought maybe he was going to give me his business card. To my great astonishment, he pulled out ten one-hundred-dollar bills in American money and handed them to me. "I want to help you with this project," he said. Then he turned, and just as suddenly as he had come, walked out of the room.

A thousand dollars!

American money!

In Guangzhou, China!

It took a moment for what had just happened to sink in. When it did, I jumped up and ran out of the door after the man. I still had his money in my hand. "Sir," I asked, when I had caught up to him, "Who are you? And why have you done this?"

He was reluctant to tell me his name, saying only that he was led of the Lord to do it. He told me that his ancestors had come from Hawaii, so I gave him the name "Peter from Hawaii."

As I tucked the money safely away, I felt that it was a down payment on things to come, a sign from God that He would supply all our needs as we endeavored to help the Chinese people. Although Peter from Hawaii had given me the money, it was from God's hand. It was money from Heaven!

Chapter 14

Pigs and Songs from God

As Geri and I were planning our second trip to China in 1994, the Lord told me to go to Indonesia for three days after we finished our work in China. Church meetings were scheduled there for us — morning, noon and night. Our airline tickets were routed as follows: Dallas, Tokyo, Beijing, Singapore, Jakarta, Tokyo, Dallas. After spending about ten days in surgery and teaching in Beijing, we would fly to Singapore for a day, then to Indonesia for the three days of meetings, then back to Tokyo and on back to Dallas. We had purchased our tickets in advance, and all our seats were preassigned.

When we arrived at the airport in Dallas for departure, we noticed that the lady at the ticket counter was spending a lot of time checking and rechecking our tickets, entering things into the computer and reading the information on her terminal. She worked for a long time without saying a word to us, and we wondered what could be taking her so long. Finally, as it was growing closer to departure time, she said to us, "Your travel agent forgot to confirm your tickets, and all your reservations have been cancelled. I'm trying to re-book them now."

I thought it would surely be a miracle if she could re-book all those same flights at the last minute for the same price. I prayed as I stood there and remembered the promise of Romans 8:28, a verse I often quote to myself at times like these:

And we know that all things work together for good to them that love God, to them who are the called according to his purpose.

Romans 8:28

I did not know how the Lord would work this situation out for our good, but I knew He would. That was His promise.

Finally the ticket agent said, "I have gotten you re-booked on all the flights."

Whew! That was good news!

"But," she continued, "I could not get you any of the same seats you had." (They had been window seats.)

Uh-oh! we thought. Bad news! It would be a thirteen-and-a-half-hour flight from Dallas to Tokyo nonstop, and I had huge notebooks full of work to do in preparation for the detailed lectures I was to give in Beijing on phacoemulsification. The only seats she had found for us were sandwiched between other people in the middle section of the big 747 jet. How was I going to find room to do all that work I had planned?

An agent at the gate told us that we could stand at the gate until everyone had boarded, and if anyone failed to show up and their assigned seat was in a better location, we could take it. The thought came to me that perhaps we could upgrade to business class, where I would have more room to work, and I asked the gate agent how much this would cost. When he quoted me the charge (several thousand dollars), I quickly dismissed this as a possibility. So we stood and waited until every last person boarded the plane, hoping for a better seat.

As it turned out, everyone showed up for the flight that day, so we had no choice but to take the crowded seats in the middle section. I decided to make the best of the situation, and I unfolded one of my notebooks and began working while the plane was still on the ground.

After a few minutes, one of the flight attendants came over and knelt down in the aisle near my seat. He leaned over and whispered to me, "Aren't you Dr. Vaughan?"

I told him I was.

He said, "You operated on my eyes a few years ago, and now I see so great! Would you like to move up to first class?"

I got my books closed and jumped out of that seat in a flash. Geri was right behind me as we followed him to the front row of the first class section. He seated me by the window on one side and Geri by the window on the other side.

What huge seats! I sank into the soft leather, looked out the window and thanked my sweet Jesus for supplying all of our needs *"according to His riches in glory"* (Philippians 4:19). He is so sweet, so wonderful, so full of good surprises.

Romans 8:28 proved true again! The Lord had worked out the details of the situation for my good. A cancelled coach seat had turned into the best first-class seat on the plane.

I worked on my spacious tray table for about ten hours straight, then put my books away and enjoyed the movie of my choice on my private TV monitor. Meanwhile, I was fed shrimp cocktail, filet mignon and a variety of other delectables, topped off with a hot fudge sundae made with Haagen-Dazs ice cream and, finally, an individual box of Godiva chocolates. One could get used to this kind of treatment very easily!

Happy Talk

Upon arriving in Beijing, I was immediately put to work teaching Chinese doctors modern cataract surgery. I performed surgery to show them, and then they performed surgeries, under my supervision, to learn. We were in surgery together from early morning until late evening — day in and day out.

111

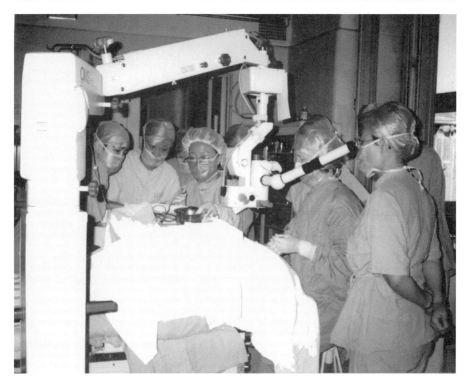

Being intently observed during surgery by Chinese doctors in Beijing, 1994.

Before going, I had requested that I be taken to a rural medical facility sometime during my stay, so one day we had no scheduled surgery. Instead, we were driven to a county hospital and then beyond that to a rural hospital. The farther we got from the big city, the worse the medical conditions became. In my heart and mind I had a strong desire to reach out to the people of the rural areas of China with good eye care. Many of them were too poor to afford surgery, so I wanted to be able to offer it to them free of charge. Some rural Chinese had gone blind as a result of poor quality surgery done on them in years gone by, and many of them were understandably afraid to have their eyes operated on — even if they were legally blind.

At the rural hospital, I asked to see the surgery room. When the doctor took me there, I noticed that everything was covered with dust, as if it had not been used in a long time. I asked him if they had the capability of sterilizing instruments. He said yes and took me outside, across a courtyard, to a three-sided lean-to. There he pointed to a black pot under which you could build a fire and said that is where they sterilized instruments. Immediately I realized that it would be impossible to do eye surgery under these conditions. Our microsurgical instruments would be ruined after one "sterilization" in the big black pot.

The only way I could envision getting the proper eye care to these rural areas was with a mobile surgery unit. This way we could create as sterile an environment as possible. We could equip the unit with an operating microscope, which is absolutely essential to eye surgery, and with a video monitor so other doctors could watch us do the surgery and learn modern techniques. I began talking about this concept with everyone I met. I told our friends. I told the doctors. I talked about the need for a mobile surgery unit morning, noon and night. Somehow there must be a way to make this dream come true.

For several days, a song had been going over and over inside of me, but I had been too busy to pay any attention to it. One day, back at the hospital in Beijing, while I was waiting for the nurses to prepare the next patient, I stood looking out a window. The song was still there. What was that song anyway?

I began to concentrate on the song and realized it was from the movie South Pacific. I had not seen that movie in decades. Why in the world was this song going on continually inside of me here in China? What were the words to that song? I tried to remember. Slowly they began to come to me:

"Talk, keep talk, keep talkin, happy talk.
Talk about all the things you do.

If you don't have a dream,
When you don't have a dream,
How you gonna make a dream come true?"

Yes, that was it. In the movie, the mother of the Polynesian girl had been singing it to the young couple by the waterfall. But those words were also true for China and for now.

I had to laugh out loud as I reflected on all my talking about my dream. The Holy Spirit has such a wonderful sense of humor, and He is right one hundred percent of the time. Yes, I had been talking, and I knew He wanted me to continue talking about my dream of a mobile surgery unit — until that dream became a reality. After all, if you don't have a dream, "how you gonna make a dream come true?"

Six Jade Pigs

The last days of surgery came, and we squeezed in as many patients as the time permitted. I went home exhausted every night, and I am sure the Chinese doctors did as well.

They were difficult days. The equipment was new to the Chinese, and the particular brand of equipment we used was unfamiliar to me. Sometimes the equipment failed to work properly, and this further complicated things.

Since the Chinese doctors were doing their first cases with this equipment, the surgery was slow and tedious and often very tense, trying to prevent complications caused by inexperienced hands.

Then there was the language barrier, which always complicates things. In one particular case, I kept telling a certain doctor, "Stop! Stop! Stop!" when I saw that he was about to get into serious trouble. He apparently did not understand the English word "stop," and kept right on going. Fortunately we were able to avoid a tragedy.

Much to my amazement, the news of my coming had spread far and wide, and people came from all parts of China, wanting me personally to do their surgery. Some of their cases were very complicated. One lady had undergone three previous surgeries on her eye, and she still could not see. She was hoping I could do her surgery and give her back her eyesight.

One little boy had suffered an accident in which scissors were stuck in his eye. By the time he came to me, he had a bad cataract on that eye and a lot of scar tissue. His family was hoping I could repair the damage.

Another patient was a man who rode a train for three or four days and nights all the way from southwest China to come to Beijing for me to do surgery on him. I was not sure how all these people knew I was going to be there, but I was determined to do my best to help them.

As I was rushing to change out of my scrubs and into my street clothes at the end of the final day of surgery, however, one of the doctors stopped me and said there was a lady begging for me to do her surgery. She had been on the list of those we wanted to help, but time had run out before we could get to her. He had explained to her that I was already late for a big farewell banquet and would not be able to do the surgery that night, but he wondered if I would be willing to come to the hospital early the next morning before my 10:00 a.m. flight, to do surgery on this woman. I could not refuse.

The banquet that night was grand. Though we were all tired, we were very happy with what had been accomplished in ten days. The hospital administrator sat at the head of the round table. As honored guests, Geri was seated to his left, and I was seated to his right.

We were served dish after dish, many of them in individual servings, and others placed in large dishes in the center of the table. We did not know what most of the food was, but it did not matter. We ate politely what was placed before us, being sure to at least taste everything,

When one individual dish of some sort was served to each of us, Geri's portion seemed different from all the rest — whatever it was. It was a flat round piece of something about half an inch thick, served on a small flat dish. Geri's portion looked more like a humped-up something.

She certainly did not want to be rude, but she was very curious about this humped-up thing sitting before her. She took the edge of the dish in her hand and began turning it to get a look at this thing from a different angle, hoping to determine what it might be. As she turned the dish, she suddenly yelled and jumped backward. (How polite could that be?).

I turned to see what was happening and saw that the head of an eel was staring her in the face. Its mouth was open, and its teeth exposed. If there is one thing in this world that Geri hates, it is snakes. She despises them. She is petrified of them. And here was the cousin of a snake sitting within striking distance of her. She was so frightened by this discovery that she nearly fell backward out of her chair trying to get away from it.

Everyone had a big laugh about all this — except Geri. She was wondering why they had done this to her. As it turns out, the head of the eel was considered to be the greatest delicacy available, so it had been given to Geri to honor her.

Seeing how this had frightened Geri, the administrator took the plate of eel from in front of her and offered it to me. I, too, declined the honor and suggested that he have it himself. He gobbled it down with great delight. It was his favorite part of the meal.

The next morning, bright and early, I went to the hospital to do that final surgery. I was surprised to find the room full of Chinese

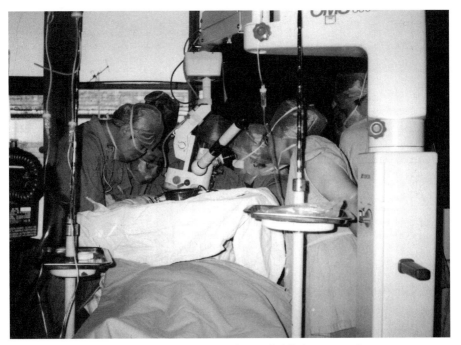

Chinese eye surgeons intently watching me do difficult surgery, 1994.

doctors wanting to watch. With all we had done over the past ten days, I wondered why this case held such special interest for them. Soon I understood.

The lady had undergone two previous glaucoma surgeries, one from the top of the eye and one from the bottom. A thin layer of scar tissue had grown into her eye, covering everything. There were tears in her iris (the colored part of the eye) and a very dense cataract was also present. This was a very complicated case.

In addition to her considerable anatomic problems, the phacoemulsification machine kept malfunctioning as I worked that morning.

I was also down to the last of the intraocular lens implants I had brought from America. They had been donated from various sources, and most of them had been of excellent quality. The only one I had left of the proper corrective power for this woman, however, was of some strange design I had never seen before. It had very long curved arms on it like the whiskers on a catfish. After the difficult job of peeling off the scar tissue and removing a dense cataract with a malfunctioning machine, I now had the dubious task of getting this catfish-like lens into this woman's eye with the limited instruments that were available.

Over and over, I tried to get the first "whisker" into the proper place in the eye, and everyone was hanging over the table, trying to see how I was going to accomplish this feat. The strange lens did not seem to want to go into the right place, and I had no instrument to put it there.

I had been praying throughout the case, realizing that only Jesus could make this blind lady see, and this complication made my prayer even more urgent. I needed God's help to get these "catfish whiskers" properly placed in the eye.

When the surgery was successfully completed, I was drained. I had poured everything that was within me into trying to make that lady see again. It was the worst case I had ever seen in thirty years of doing eye surgery, and I was thanking God that it was, at long last, over.

Before I left that day, the Chinese doctor in charge of the lady's case said she wanted to give me something and asked if I could please stop by her room on my way out of the building. When I went to her room, she handed me a small box and indicated (through the interpreter) that she wanted me to open it right then. Inside the box were six jade pigs. She explained that the number six meant "very good," and since the next year would be "the year of the pig," she had chosen six jade pigs as a gift of appreciation for me.

I thanked her kindly for the pigs. I loved them. When I got back to Dallas, I put them on a table by my private office entrance so that every time I would go in and out of that door I would see the pigs

Six jade pigs, gift from a grateful Chinese lady.

and be reminded to pray for that lady. I knew I had done my best for her, but I also knew that it would take a miracle from God to make her eye see clearly again.

On my next trip back to China, in 1995, I got a call one night from the head of the Ophthalmology Department at the hospital. He seemed very excited and wanted to come to my hotel right then. When he arrived, he unfolded a newspaper with an article in it written by the lady who have given me the jade pigs. The article was in Chinese, and he had to interpret it for me. The lady spoke of the amazing improvement to her vision after the surgery and went on to tell of the work we were wanting to do in rural China.

How utterly amazing! A prominent Chinese newspaper had printed a long article written by a common laboring woman with no "pull," no "special connections," and the thrust of the article was about the work of a foreigner, which was very unusual. Wonders never cease! God knows how to accomplish His works among men, and He sometimes chooses the most unlikely people to work through. The Apostle Paul wrote:

But God hath chosen the foolish things of the world to confound the wise; and God hath chosen the weak things of the world to confound the things which are mighty. And base things of the world, and things which are despised, hath God chosen, yea, and things which are not, to bring to nought things that are: That no flesh should glory in his presence.   1 Corinthians 1:27-29

The following page contains a Xerox copy of the article she wrote. Here is the English translation:

An American Doctor That I Have Met

Dear Editor:

Ms. Elizabeth Vaughan is an American eye-doctor in her fifties. She works for the Medical Center of Ophthalmology in Dallas, USA. Dr. Vaughan is full of compassion for the Chinese people. Since last year, she has visited Beijing Xie-he Medical Center of Ophthalmology twice at her own expenses, imparting advanced eye-operation techniques to Chinese doctors. During her stay in China, she also treated Chinese eye patients with great enthusiasm. Dr. Vaughan has gained extensive praises from the Chinese people.

Ultrasonic crystal emulsification extraction is an advanced technology of treating cataract. With a cut of only 3.2-millimeter, an eye-doctor can excise a cataract and graft a man-made crystal into the eye. There is no stitching involved in the operation. With this cataract extraction method, eye patients will enjoy quicker recovery of eyesight and less astigmatism afterwards. When Dr. Vaughan

健康报

● 中华人民共和国卫生部主办 ●

| 1995年 3月 | 21 星期二 | 农历乙亥年 二月二十一 | 国内统一刊号　CN11—0010　代号1—20 第 4381 期 |

编辑同志：

伊丽莎白·旺医师是一位50多岁的美国眼科女医师，在美国达拉斯眼科中心工作。她对中国人民有着诚挚的感情。去年以来，她两次自费到北京协和医院眼科传授先进的眼科手术技术，热情地为患者服务，得到了广泛的好评。

超声乳化晶体摘除术是一种治疗白内障的先进技术，仅以3.2毫米

我所遇到的美国医生

的切口就可以摘除白内障，植入人工晶体，不需要缝合伤口。手术后散光度小、视力恢复快。当伊丽莎白·旺得知在中国还没有普遍开展这项手术时，就主动提出到北京协和医院来传授这项技术。经有关部门批准，她于去年10月来北京工作了两个星期，除了讲课、录像演示、仔细地讲解这项技术的每个细节外，还亲自上手术台为患者手术。她精湛的医术令中国同行钦佩。在短短两周时间内，她亲自带教了四名中国眼科医师，使他们掌握了这项先进技术。现在，这项技术已在北京协和医院顺利地展开。

在中国工作期间，她早上总是提前到医院，中午也不休息，直到下午六点多钟，才回住所安歇。我是一名青光眼、白内障患者。在我住院期间，经历了这样一件事，去年10月13日，伊丽莎白·旺医师将要回国了。12日一整天，她要为六位病人做手术，我有幸被安排在最后一个。病人依次被叫进手术室。当我进手术室时，已是下午五时，因为伊丽莎白·旺医师晚上六点还要出席有关部门为她举行的宴会，时间已不允许她再为我做手术了。这让我很失望，只得无奈地回

到病房。但不久，我便得到通知：伊丽莎白·旺医师决定，她第二天一早，加班为我做手术。第二天，她和她的助手们早早来到医院为我手术，直到上午9时20分，手术顺利地完成了。临行前，她还坚持要到病房来看望我，然后，才放心地去赶乘中午的飞机回国。

伊丽莎白·旺医师在中国工作期间，为了帮助中国开展防盲工作，她亲自到农村了解开展白内障手术的情况。当她看到相当多的农村白内障患者得不到及时治疗时，她认真地思考如何来帮助中国农村地区的白内障盲人。经她提议和资助，一个大规模的防盲项目正在计划之中。我想不久的将来，这个项目得以实施后，将会给更多的白内障盲人送去光明。

北京瀛海棋具厂

李国玉

121

learned that this cataract extraction technique had not been spread in China yet, she volunteered to go to the Beijing Xie-he Medical Center Department of Ophthalmology to teach this technique. After the approval of the related departments, she was able to come to Beijing last October. During her two-week stay, she devoted herself to the spread of this advanced eye operation technique in China. Besides offering classes, explaining in detail every step and procedure of this operation, Dr. Vaughan also performed cataract extraction on patients. Her consummate medical skills command hearty admiration from her Chinese colleagues. In only two weeks, she imparted ultrasonic crystal emulsification extraction technique to four Chinese eye doctors. Now, this technique is being spread to others at Beijing Xie-he Medical Center.

During Dr. Vaughan's two-week stay in China, she worked very hard. She always came into the hospital early in the morning and worked through the lunch hour. She worked on until 6 o'clock in the evening.

I am a cataract and glaucoma eye patient. When I was in the Medical Center of Ophthalmology, I had a wonderful experience with Dr. Vaughan. It was last October. Dr. Vaughan had been in China for nearly two weeks, and she was going back to America on October 13. On October 12, Dr. Vaughan would perform cataract extraction operations on six eye patients. I was very fortunate to be one of those patients and was scheduled to be the last one receiving the operation. Patients were called into the operation room in order. When it was my turn, it was already 5 o'clock in the afternoon. Dr. Vaughan had to attend a farewell banquet held in her honor by various

Chinese organizations at six o'clock, and she would not have enough time to perform the operation for me. I was very disappointed.

Not long after I returned to my ward, I got a notice that Dr. Vaughan had decided to perform the operation on me the next morning right before her return flight to the United States. I was so touched by her great compassion for the patients. The next morning Dr. Vaughan and her assistants came to the hospital very early and performed the operation on me. After the operation, Dr. Vaughan insisted on visiting me in my ward, making sure everything was fine with me. Then she rushed to the airport for the flight going to the United States.

In order to launch blind-prevention programs in China's remote countryside areas, Dr. Vaughan went to the countryside herself and collected firsthand information on how to spread cataract operation techniques in the countryside. When she learned that many cataract eye patients became blind because of improper treatment, she began thinking through a plan that could help cataract patients in China's countryside. Under her proposal and sponsorship, a large-scale countryside blind prevention program is on its way. I am sure that in the very near future this program will bring light and hope to many cataract eye patients.

We thanked God for all this free promotional material. How good He is! In the years to come, many articles would appear in Chinese newspapers praising the work we were doing.

The following are excerpts from some of the letters I got from Chinese doctors that I taught during these visits to the big university hospital:

中国医学科学院

眼 科 研 究 中 心

EYE RESEARCH CENTER
Chinese Academy of Medical Sciences

Dear Dr. Vaughan:

I find an ordinary "thank you" inadequate to tell you how grateful I am for your general donation and wholehearted teaching. I have been an opthalmologist for 30 years, but I have never seen so kind a teacher as you. You worked in our operating room from 8 a.m. to 7 p.m., teaching and treating. We have learned a lot from you. A great deal of blind people have already gotten their good vision due to your help. We must all learn this kind of Bethune's spirit, that utter to devotion to others without any thought of self, which you have shown during one week period working with us. Your fantabulous job surely will be a great contribution to the cataract surgery in Beijing.

I hope you come again next year in the best season of Beijing and keep in touch with us. We always appreciate the assistance you have given.

With best regards,
Y.D., M.D.

• • •

Dear Dr. Vaughan,

I feel pain for you to leave. All my patients and I want to thank you. You are both a very nice and master-handed doctor and a

124

warmhearted teacher. I have learned a lot from you. Now I know the principle steps of phacoemulsification and I realize the importance to treat the complications during the operation in order to save the patient's vision. All of these are the result of your hard work. I appreciate your help and kindness. I hope you come back and I look forward to having the opportunity to learn from you!

Warm regards,
H.S., M.D.

● ● ●

Dear Dr. Vaughan,

As you prepare to return to the United States, it gives me a great deal of pleasure to write you, on behalf of the Department of Ophthalmology, Peking Union Medical College Hospital, and my colleague, and in my own name, to express our appreciation for your generous help. During two weeks, you performed the cataract surgery and taught us the endolenticular phacoemulsification and the foldable intraocular lens implantation. I and my colleague learned a lot from you. Without your help, we could not possibly have a good grasp of the technique of the phacoemulsification and the foldable intraocular lens implantation.
I am also moved by your noble idea of giving more help to the poor blind in the rural areas of China. All you have done in our department developed and expanded such friendly links of the ophthalmologists and people between China and the United States. As you know, I enjoy an especially close relationship with you. I welcome you to visit our department again. The warmest welcome from me and my colleagues awaits you whenever.

With the best of wishes to you and your family,

J.Z., M.D.

Chapter 15

My Burden for
the Rural Areas of China

We had met up with Ruth and Susan in Beijing, and Susan suggested that we go to Xian in western China to see the terra-cotta warriors recently discovered outside the city by a farmer digging a well on his farm. What he found was truly amazing. Over the past

The terra-cotta soldiers near Xian, China, 1994.

The terra-cotta soldiers near Xian, China, 1994.

The terra-cotta soldiers near Xian, China, 1994.

several years they had unearthed more and more of the life-sized soldiers. Each of them had been painted in bright colors, and each had his sword or spear or bow and arrows.

One of the most amazing things about these terra-cotta warriors was that each of the approximately six thousand soldiers, found standing in columns, had a distinctive face, beard and hair style, and there was an immediate and recognizable distinction between the officers within their ranks. This huge terra-cotta army had been buried with Emperor Qin Shihuang around 220 B.C. in the hope that it could guard him beyond the grave and aid in his quest for immortality. The huge underground room that had become their vault had remained hidden for centuries. What an unforgettable sight that was!

After we viewed this ancient marvel, Geri decided to go back to the hotel room, while the rest of us pressed on to see more of the local sights. While she was alone in the room, she looked out the

With Ruth and Susan, Xian, China, 1994.

window at the great mass of humanity living in Xian and began to pray for them. Suddenly the Lord spoke to her, confirming that He had called us to the Chinese people. It was thrilling for her to hear the voice of the Lord solidify once more what we had long believed to be true.

When the three of us returned to the hotel, Geri was still standing by the window. Ruth sat down on the arm of a chair nearby and began singing a little song:

> *Oh come and go with Me*
> *To My little corner of the world.*
> *Stay awhile with Me*
> *In My little corner of the world.*
> *I always knew*
> *I'd find someone like you.*
> *So welcome to*
> *My little corner of the world.*
>
> *And if you care to stay*
> *In My little corner of the world.*
> *Then we could hide away*
> *In My little corner of the world.*
> *You'd soon forget*
> *There's any other place.*
> *So welcome to*
> *My little corner of the world.*

The three of us had no knowledge of what the Lord had been telling Geri that day, but it was essentially the same message as the words to this song. Ruth, flowing in the Holy Ghost as usual, had just sung a confirmation from the heart of God to Geri, who was now in tears.

There is nothing more wonderful in life than to watch the Lord work — in small, personal ways, as well as large nation-shaking ways. Jesus said that our Father knows how many hairs are on our head. He guards us as the pupil of His eye. His love for us is unfathomable. He has planted roses all along our walk of life, like this little song for Geri on a dusty day in Xian.

On our way back to the airport, we visited the huge wall that surrounds the city of Xian. It is as wide as a city street. We walked up the steep steps to the top of the wall, and there we found Chinese merchants selling their wares. I was not interested in buying, I was interested in looking, so I walked to the edge of the wall and looked down on the city.

Everything seemed to be gray. The sky was gray. The roofs of the houses were gray. The leaves of the trees were gray. The streets and ground were gray. I was told that the winds blow across the Mongolian steppes, picking up dirt from them and filling the air with the dust. This dust is then deposited on literally everything.

In addition, the people of Xian heat and cook by burning coal,

A truck washing the leaves of the trees, as seen from the wall around Xian, China, 1994.

and the smoke of it adds to the grayness of the atmosphere and the surroundings. I noticed a water truck driving slowly down the street. A man in the back of the truck had a long hose and, with it, was trying to spray the leaves of the trees. When he had passed, we could see a little of the true green color of the leaves, until the wind blew more dust that way.

My interesting viewing was interrupted when Geri brought a Chinese woman over to meet me. She had been selling goods on the wall and had begun speaking to Geri in fairly good English. She said she was a nurse and had several doctors in her family, so Geri thought we would enjoy talking. She introduced herself as Deborah and proceeded to tell me that her father was a doctor who had a private clinic in Xian. This surprised me greatly, since I did not know there was such a thing as private medicine in China.

We did not have much time to spend on the wall that day because we had a plane to catch, so our conversation with Deborah was brief. Someone took our picture together, Deborah quickly wrote down

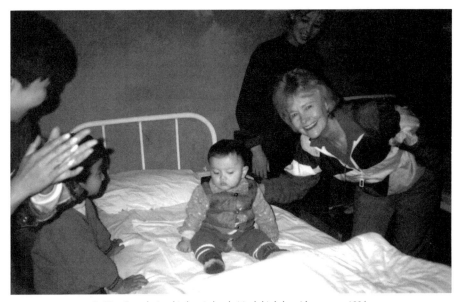

In Xian, I taught in a big hospital and visited this baby with cataracts, 1994.

her address, and I told her I would send her a copy of the picture. Later she told me that she never dreamed I would actually write to her or send her the picture. She was so happy that I had, and we began to correspond.

I was very impressed with the quality of the English in Deborah's letters. We became friends, and began to make plans for me to visit her family clinic on my next trip to China.

By the time I returned to Xian in September of 1994, to teach in a large hospital, I was amazed at two things about Deborah. First, her oral English had improved remarkably in the short six-month period since our last meeting. Secondly, she had gotten a book of ophthalmology terms in English and Chinese and had been memorizing them — why, I wasn't sure. It did not seem to serve any useful purpose in her life, yet it was something she wanted to do.

I met Deborah's father (a retired pediatrician, who had started his own small clinic after finishing his required period of government service), her mother (a retired pharmacist who had opened a small pharmacy in conjunction with her husband's pediatric clinic) and her brother (a urologist, also working at a clinic). They were all very kind and sweet, but none of them spoke English except Deborah.

Deborah seemed so eager to learn English and ophthalmology that I sent her a home-study course for ophthalmic assistants when I got back to America. By this time I knew that God had work for us to do in China, and I was wondering if Deborah was to be a part of that work. I did not yet know how all of this would fit together. I would wait and watch the Lord weave it according to His good pleasure.

In time, as I pondered our ongoing work in China, I realized how useful it would be to have a bilingual surgical assistant trained in modern ophthalmic surgery. Such a person could help in teaching

Chicken feet, a delicacy, Xian, China.

Chinese doctors and nurses in the future because he or she would have no language barrier. I came to the conclusion that the only way to properly train such a person would be to bring him or her to America for a period of on-the-job training.

The more I thought on this, the more Deborah came to mind. Since she had no telephone, I wrote her a letter and asked her to call me at a pre-designated time. When I asked her on the phone if she would like to come to America to study ophthalmic nursing, she could not believe her ears. She asked me to repeat the question because she thought she had not understood me correctly. Coming to America had been, for her, something completely beyond hoping for. She had never dreamed of anything so wonderful.

After Deborah took a little time to discuss my invitation with her family, she contacted me again to say that she would love to come. I told her to get a passport in Xian and a visa at the American Embassy in Beijing. She could then return to America with us on our next trip into China. This all sounded very simple at the time, but I could never have anticipated how very difficult it would actually be.

We met Deborah in Beijing on our next trip into China. It was the third day before we were to leave to return to America. I was surprised to learn that she had been refused a visa at the American embassy. She had been told that she would have to return to her hometown (a two-day train ride from Beijing) and get certified copies of her school diplomas, marriage license, work history and other such papers. To do all this would have taken weeks, and we didn't have that much time.

I told Deborah not to worry, that we would go with her to the embassy the next day and God would make a way for her to get the necessary visa.

"No! No!" she protested. "I can't go back there until I get all these certified documents."

I again assured her that God could make a way where there now seemed to be no way. We would get a visa.

The next day we were at the American embassy with Deborah bright and early (around 8:00 a.m.). Because we were American citizens, they let us in before the masses of waiting Chinese, and we took Deborah with us. As it turned out, we were the first ones in the embassy. The doors had not yet opened to the public. We presented our passports and signed Deborah in to be interviewed.

When the consular officers arrived for work, they began calling out the names of those they would interview, but Deborah was not among them. As the morning progressed, and they kept calling out other names, but she still was not called.

Finally, about 10:00 a.m., I stepped up to one of the windows and asked if they could tell me when Deborah would be called. The clerk explained to me that this was Deborah's second visit to the embassy, and they did not see returning applicants until 1:00 p.m. I said we had not been aware of this policy, but that we would go get some lunch and accomplish some other things and then come back at one. Then he informed us that our passports would not be returned to us if we left. (They had taken our passports when we entered the embassy.) It seemed that we were stuck in the U.S. Embassy, so we sat back down with all the Chinese who were waiting to be seen, and we waited.

When all the interviews were finished and the applicants had cleared out of the room, we stayed in our places. The embassy staff went to lunch and left us there waiting alone. We were still there waiting when they resumed their places at 1:00 p.m. As more applicants were let in, the officers began calling more names.

As name after name was called, we were disturbed to find that Deborah was not among them. About 2:30 p.m. I stepped up to a window again and asked when Deborah would be called. They didn't know, I was told. Everything was done on a random basis. They had no control over it. We waited, and we waited some more.

It was nearly four o'clock when Deborah's name was finally called. I went to the window with her. The officer looked over her papers and told her that he could not grant the visa she was applying for.

I explained to the gentleman why Deborah was applying for the visa, that we were going to have mobile surgery units to do surgery on poor blind people in the Chinese countryside and that Deborah needed to come to America to train as an ophthalmic surgical nurse for this project. He asked me what proof I could present of the existence of the project.

This shocked me, as it never occurred to me that I would be asked for proof of what I was saying. I did have documents, I told him, but I had not brought them with me, and the next day was our last day in Beijing. He finally suggested that an appointment be set up for us with his boss the next day, and it would be up to the boss to decide Deborah's fate.

As we left the embassy that afternoon, I told Deborah that God must want me to meet the boss of the embassy, and this was His way of getting me in there to meet him. I told her not to be discouraged, that God would get her a visa. Even though we had to spend our whole day sitting in the waiting room without food or drink, I somehow knew that God was in all of this. His ways are higher than our ways.

That night I called the head of the ophthalmology department where I had been teaching and asked him to make me copies of all the documents related to our mobile surgery units. The next day I showed all these documents to the consular officer and told him about wanting to bring hope to those sitting in darkness. He listened politely and then said he would give Deborah a visa. He would also set up a file on us so that if we wanted to bring any other Chinese to America in the future, they, too, could get a visa more easily.

We left the embassy that day jubilant and in awe of the ways of God. He had done *"exceeding abundantly above all that we ask or think, according to the power that worketh in us"* (Ephesians 3:20).

I knew that Deborah had received her visa by the hand of God, but I did not realize the extent of the miracle until several years later — when I was trying to get a visa for someone else. It was explained to me on this occasion that those who receive visas are those who have concrete reasons to return to China. For example, I was told, visas are granted to people who have lucrative businesses in China and would not want to leave them and move to America. As much as possible, visa officers are looking for assurances that the person applying for a visitor's visa to America, will return to China. If no such assurance exists, they rarely give a visa.

Deborah was in the very worst category. She spoke good English and, as a nurse, could easily find work in America. There was only one reason Deborah got a visa, and His name is Jesus.

After Deborah came to America and we had time to talk, I found out some interesting things about her life in China. When she was a small child, the country had gone through some very difficult times, when food was scarce and many Chinese were starving to death. Although she was only six years old, she had to go before sunup each morning and stand in line to get food for her elderly grandparents, to keep them alive.

When Deborah was in the fifth grade, schools were closed because of the Cultural revolution. She was separated from her family and sent to the countryside with other children to do farm work with the peasants. She had slept on a bed of mud and done hard manual labor.

At fourteen years of age, Deborah joined the army, where she was trained as a nurse. This also had not been an easy life.

As a young adult, Deborah had a strong desire to learn English. Despite the curtailment of her formal education, she was determined to continue learning. She signed up for night classes and watched television programs that taught English. She got books and studied long hours on her own.

She was not sure why she had such a desire to learn English. Beyond speaking the language, she had no further goals in mind. It was a driving force within her, but where it would lead she did not know. This desire to learn English was so strong that she left her nursing job and began to sell things to tourists on the wall at Xian. By speaking with tourists, she reasoned, she could improve her English. She had made this job move just two months before the fateful day we met her on the wall.

In retrospect, Deborah realizes that it was God who gave her the desire to learn English so that He could use her life for the purpose He designed. After meeting us on the wall and learning about Jesus, she gave her life to Christ and now serves Him diligently.

Yes, He loves us before we know Him, and He is molding and shaping us for His use — even before we yield our lives to Him.

The Great Light

On one of my trips to Xian, I was left alone in the hotel room, while my traveling companions — Geri, Susan and Ruth — were off seeing some of the sights. I knelt beside the bed and began to pray. As I prayed, I had a vision of a Chinese man sitting on the floor with his arms around his bent legs and his head down on his knees. He was in total darkness and hopelessness. He was blind, so his world was black, and he had no hope whatsoever that his situation would ever change. All the days of his life, he was sure, he would sit in blackness until the day he died.

I had never felt hopelessness before, but I felt this man's hopelessness. It was a feeling too horrible to describe. I began to weep for him, as I felt what he was feeling. Then suddenly the Word of the Lord came like a bolt of lightning into the pitch-black darkness:

The people which sat in darkness saw great light.
Matthew 4:16

My tears turned to rejoicing, and I knew in an instant that God would bring both physical and spiritual light to these people who were sitting in darkness. He would make a way for us to treat the eye diseases (cataracts, glaucoma, myopia, etc.) of the people in rural China, many of whom were very poor and had no eye care at all. And He would make a way for the light of the Gospel of Jesus Christ to be shed abroad in their hearts.

Isaiah had prophesied of Jesus, the Great Light, seven hundred years before the birth of Christ:

The people that walked in darkness have seen a great light: they that dwell in the land of the shadow of death, upon them hath the light shined. Isaiah 9:2

Now, nearly two thousand years after Christ first shined His light among men, He was still shining it brightly into dark hearts. He had not changed:

Jesus Christ the same yesterday, and to day, and for ever. Hebrews 13:8

When the others returned to the hotel, I shared with them the vision I had and the joyful solution the Lord had given. Geri shared with us a time when she had seen that great light of Jesus. It was in 1972, and she was passing through a period of severe difficulty in her life. She had been lying on her living room sofa, crying out to God in the night, when she saw a distant light like a star that began coming closer and closer to her. The closer it came, the larger and brighter it became, until she recognized the very person of Jesus in the light.

Actually, she realized, the light was the glory emanating from Jesus. If He moved His arm, the glory would move, staying around His body. The glory shone through the nail holes in His hands. She wanted so badly to go with Him and stay with Him — never to be separated from that glorious Jesus. He stretched out His arms to her and said, "Not yet, but soon." Then He said, "Acts 26:16" and disappeared. Hurriedly she found her Bible and looked up the passage in the book of Acts.

But rise, and stand upon thy feet: for I have appeared unto thee for this purpose, to make thee a minister and a witness both of these things which thou hast seen, and of those things in the which

I will appear unto thee; Delivering thee from the people, and from the Gentiles, unto whom now I send thee, TO OPEN THEIR EYES, AND TO TURN THEM FROM DARKNESS TO LIGHT, and from the power of Satan unto God, that they may receive forgiveness of sins, and inheritance among them which are sanctified by faith that is in me.   Acts 26:16-18

These were words spoken by Jesus to Paul on the road to Damascus. Jesus had appeared to him at midday with a light brighter than the brightness of the sun. Paul later said of that experience:

At midday, O king, I saw in the way a light from heaven, above the brightness of the sun shining round about me and them which journeyed with me.   Acts 26:13

We cannot imagine a light brighter than the sun at noon on a cloudless day, but the light of Jesus made the sunlight look dim. At His light, every knee shall bow and every tongue will confess that Jesus Christ is Lord. He IS *"the light of the world."*

Now, Geri, a nonmedical person, was on a mission to open peoples' eyes and *"turn them from darkness to light,"* just as Jesus said she would twenty-two years before. We do not have to know HOW God will accomplish His word, we simply trust that He WILL do it. So we continue to go into dark places, trusting that He will make the great light of His presence shine abroad and dispel the darkness.

Gangu

The strong desire in my heart to reach out to the poor people in the rural areas that needed eye surgery did not diminish. The vision of the blind man sitting in blackness and hopelessness burned in my soul. I had to do something, so I asked a Chinese friend to make arrangements for us to go to a particularly poor area of China and do free surgery. She arranged for us to go to a remote place called Gangu.

There were five members in our team: LuLu (my scrub nurse), Deborah (my circulating nurse), Austin (LuLu's husband), Geri and me. The first three, of course, were native Chinese who had been given English names. To get to Gangu, we had to fly from Beijing to Lanzhou in western China and then take a six-hour train ride. City officials met our train and took us to a factory dormitory to stay, since there were no hotels in the town. The people had never seen Westerners, and our presence created quite a stir.

Early the next morning we were taken to the local hospital and to a very small room, about the size of the average American household bathroom. This was the examining room, and I saw that it had a slit lamp (a machine used for examining eyes).

People were lined up, pushing and shoving, to be first to get into the small room for me to examine their eyes. Somehow they had heard that I would be there, and they had walked into Gangu from all the remote areas around. I began to see patients as fast as I could. Everyone I saw needed surgery. I wrote their names on a legal pad, and the pad filled up fast. How would it be possible to do surgery on so many people in the short time I had available?

About then things got a whole lot more complicated. I suddenly realized that the suitcase I had brought — filled with my surgical instruments, suture material, intraocular lenses and medications — was locked and that the key had been left in the dormitory room. I asked Geri and Austin to go back to the room and bring me the key. Somehow the two of them managed to push their way out of that small room, past the crowds (which were growing by the minute), and get out of the hospital.

My Burden for the Rural Areas of China

Leaving the train station in Lanzhou to go to Gangu. With Lu Lu, Austin, Geri and Deborah, 1996.

A street scene in Gangu, China, 1996.

A man playing a native musical instrument, Lanzhou, China

A sidewalk medical clinic, Gangu, China, 1996.

A grandfather bringing his grandson home from
a trip to the market, Gangu, China, 1996.

I was surprised by the tenacity of the people. Little old ladies who looked weak to me were shoving with all their might, trying to get into that room, as if their very life depended on it. They must have felt that this was the only chance they would ever have to see again. Here was a real-life depiction of the hopelessness I had seen in the vision, yet our presence had ignited a spark of hope.

The Chinese doctors were trying to keep the door to the tiny examining room shut so we would not be crushed, but the crowd outside in the hospital hallway far outnumbered them. Anytime the door would be opened just a small crack, more people would force their way into the room. This was the circumstance Geri and Austin faced when they returned to the hospital with the suitcase key.

The two of them worked and worked and worked some more, trying to get through the crowd and back into the room. At one point, Geri was so tightly jammed up against a wall that she was afraid she might die right then and there. If it had not been for Austin, who was young and strong, Geri probably would have been injured severely. Finally, they worked their way into the room with the key.

Geri's face was ashen, and I noticed that she kept standing by the third-story window and looking out for about fifteen minutes. I asked her, "Why do you keep looking out the window?" She said she was trying to decide which route would give her the best chance of survival if the crowd got totally out of control: jumping out of the third-floor window onto the concrete below or going back out into the hallway, where she had nearly been crushed to death.

Before long, Geri said she could not stand to stay in that hospital any longer. She was too shaken by the experience. She somehow had to get out and get back to the room. She decided to pretend that she was sick so that the crowds would let her through. Her plan worked, and Austin took her back to her room, but she shook the rest of the day. Had it not been for the grace of God, this episode might well have ended Geri's usefulness as a missionary to the Chinese countryside. She would recover from it.

Deborah, LuLu and I were left in the hospital with the thousands of people needing surgery. One very old lady, about four feet tall, stood in front of me and kept saying some word like, "Sista! Sista!" I did not know what she was talking about until she grabbed the jade cross I had around my neck and kissed it and made the sign of the cross, pointing to herself. I realized she had been, at one time, a Catholic nun, and she was trying to tell me she was a "sister." I decided I would definitely do surgery on that lady — even though I would not have time to care for most of the people that came.

When my list of people needing surgery was already far too long for the time I had available, I told the Chinese doctors to tell the remaining crowd of people to go home. For whatever reason, they were afraid to do it, so I stood up on a chair myself and made hand gestures, as I said, "No more! No more! Go home!"

No one moved, so I took my big suitcase full of surgical supplies and proceeded to walk out of the little examining room. The people parted like the waters of the Red Sea, and I walked through their midst straight on to surgery — where my next adventure was waiting.

As we have seen, modern eye surgery is microscopic surgery, and it is imperative to have a good microscope to see what you are doing. Some of the tissue that we deal with has to be sewn at a depth

"Sister" awaiting eye surgery in Gangu with a local doctor, trying to help, 1996.

of microns. So, as soon as we got to the operating room I asked to see the operating microscope.

At first I was told that they had none. Then, they said they did have one — in the corner, but it had not been used in more than ten years.

"Why has it not been used?" I asked.

"Because we could not see through it," was the reply.

I asked to see it anyway, knowing that I could not do surgery at all without some sort of magnification. When they brought out the microscope, and I took one look through it, my heart sank. It was like looking through a glass smeared with Vaseline. You could only see the vague outline of things.

What to do? I had no choice. I could either use this terrible Vaseline-like microscope or not do any surgery at all. I decided to forge ahead and do the best I could.

The Chinese doctors asked me what kind of suture I wanted, and I asked them to show me what they had. They had two kinds: black or white. Both looked like fishing line for a deep sea expedition. I graciously declined the fishing-line suture and pulled out the beautiful 10-0 nylon I had brought with me. We were all set to start the procedures.

As I tried very hard to do a good job — without being able to see well exactly what I was doing — I had to rely primarily on the Great Physician, Jesus, to do what I could not do and see what I could not see. I was grateful for twenty-six years of experience in eye surgery which had taught me where things were supposed to be — whether I could see them or not.

We did case after case without stopping, until LuLu was about to faint from lack of nourishment. I had some chocolate candy in my bag, so I gave her two pieces, and we kept on going. We did not eat a meal or drink all day. We had to make the most of every moment, for the time was short, and the need was great.

A beautiful baby in Gangu, 1996.

By the time night had fallen, we still had not gotten to the "sister's" name on the list, so I told them to get her ready next. We operated on "sister" that night and thanked God for the opportunity to take care of one of His little sheep — in addition to caring for all the others that He loved — even though many of them did not yet know Him. We finished "sister's" surgery at about 9:30 p.m., and everyone was exhausted.

When I came out of the operating room, there was a group of people still there waiting for me to check their eyes. Most of the others had gone away, but a group of the most critical had remained, waiting all day to be seen. (And we Americans complain if we have to wait even an hour to see a doctor.)

By the time I finished seeing those patients and they drove me back to the dormitory, it was nearly midnight. Much to my surprise, all the dignitaries from the City of Gangu had been waiting for my arrival to have a banquet. I was really too tired to eat, but I smiled and ate anyway. Geri and Austin met us there. Geri was still shaking from her traumatic experience at the clinic.

As I reflect back on Gangu, I can see again the desperation in the faces of the people, the longing in their eyes. It breaks my heart to think of even one sitting there in blackness and hopelessness. Oh Lord, send us back soon to bring sight to the blind, to bring light where there is darkness, to let them see Jesus!

He said:

> *The Spirit of the Lord is upon me, because he hath anointed me to preach the gospel to the poor; he hath sent me to heal the broken-hearted, to preach deliverance to the captives, and RECOVERY OF SIGHT TO THE BLIND, to set at liberty them that are bruised, to preach the acceptable year of the Lord* [the day when salvation and the free favors of God profusely abound, Amplified].
>
> Luke 4:18-19

May we be His light in this dark world.

Chapter 16

Glory Eye Center Becomes A Reality

I continued to dream my dream of mobile surgery units reaching far out into the remote areas of the Chinese countryside, doing free eye surgery on poor people who had no care. The only hindrance to its implementation was the lack of funds to buy the units and equip them.

When I returned to China in September of 1994 to teach modern cataract surgery and observed that people were coming from all parts of China wanting me personally to do their surgery, this planted the thought in my mind. If we could open a state-of-the-art eye surgery center in Beijing, there would be plenty of people willing and able to pay for excellent surgery. Such a surgery center could generate revenue to create and operate mobile surgery units. I began to work toward this goal.

There were many roadblocks along the way. A foreigner could not build a medical facility in China, for instance, so I would need a Chinese partner. I tried to work with a large hospital in Beijing. They liked the idea but could not seem to implement it. For several years I continued to talk about this dream to all my Chinese friends, trusting God to raise up a Chinese partner.

One night, before leaving Beijing, a friend called saying that she had just met a woman, Mrs. Wang, who was interested in being my partner and wanted to meet with me the following day. Since we were booked on a flight that was to leave Beijing the next morning, that would leave no time to meet with Mrs. Wang. This flight, however, was cancelled, and the next one would not leave until 2:00 p.m. This opened a time slot to meet Mrs. Wang. God's timing is always perfect.

At our first meeting I told Mrs. Wang my dream. She, too, had a heart to help poor people. We decided to further investigate a joint effort. She was a decisive person, one to take action. We both liked efficiency, and negotiations moved along quickly. When we came to an agreement, she came to Dallas for the signing of the final accord.

In the months that followed, two Chinese doctors, Dr. Joe and Dr. David, came to Dallas to be trained. Dr. Joe was an eye surgeon, and I worked with him week after week for four months teaching him modern cataract surgery. In the meantime, the necessary modern equipment was acquired, a building was prepared in Beijing, and the other necessary personnel were hired. Before we knew it, everything was in place for the Grand Opening of Glory Eye Center.

When I arrived in Beijing the day before the Grand Opening in February of 1998, there were three television cameras rolling, filming my every move. After being in airplanes and airports for the past twenty-four hours, I didn't feel very photogenic, but that didn't seem to bother the Chinese. It was an historic moment for them — and for us as well. How wonderful it was to see the fulfillment of our dream, the realization of our God-given desire for the people of China!

As I stepped out of the customs area, I was presented with a huge bouquet of flowers, and there were hugs all around from the Chinese I had grown to love so much.

The next day was the Grand Opening of the Center, and what a gala event it turned out to be! There was a large rainbow-colored balloon arching over the entrance of the building, confirmation that God keeps His promises. There were also large bouquets of flow-

Celebrating at Glory Eye Center, Beijing, China, 1998.

With a group of ladies who danced at the Glory Eye Center grand opening celebration, 1998.

ers all around with red banners across them. Mrs. Wang had done a fabulous job of creating an atmosphere of celebration.

There was a group of ladies, all dressed in red, who danced in the street in front of the Center to the beat of a small rhythm band. Crowds gathered to watch them and to see what all the fuss was about. Government dignitaries and heads of corporations had come, as well as my doctor friends from other hospitals where I had taught over the years. Many speeches were made over loud-speakers mounted in the streets.

Again, Chinese television crews were there, as well as representatives of local newspapers and radio stations to record the event and give us more free publicity.

After the celebration was over all the invited guests were taken to a banquet, while Dr. Joe and I entered the surgical suite to do cataract surgery. The television crews, who had stuck to me like glue, asked if they could film us doing surgery, and they did.

The seemingly endless television interviews, Beijing, China, 1999

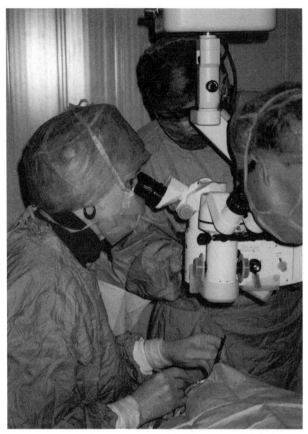

Doing surgery at Glory Eye Center, 1998.

The media coverage of our work at Glory Eye Center has amazed me from the beginning. There have been many articles written in Beijing newspapers over the years and many television specials about our work. This media coverage has been so widespread that I was told many Chinese recognize my face. When I heard this I thought it must be an exaggeration, until one day I was walking through the silk market with some friends. There were many small shops in a large open-air market. One friend was asking the price of some merchandise in one of these shops, while I was standing in the walkway, just looking around.

155

Visiting a lady, blind from cataracts, in her one-room home in rural China, 1998.
(She gave us the best she had to eat, persimmons.)

The same lady immediately after eye surgery. "I once was blind, but now I see," 1998.

The shopkeeper had quoted her a price, when he looked up and saw me. He called to me in broken English, "You eye doctor that loves Chinese people."

I said, "Yes, I love Chinese people."

Suddenly, the price of his merchandise fell drastically, and my friend came away with a real bargain. I was shocked that a common man on the street of Beijing knew me by sight and had this wonderful knowledge of my love for his people. No one could accomplish this but God, and I know that He has done it for a purpose that is as yet unseen.

Since the opening of the center, many poor people have been brought from the countryside with the help of the Red Cross, and have received free eye surgery. The story of one of the many poor people we have operated on serves to illustrate what has been accomplished. Let's call her Mrs. Zhu. I removed a cataract from Mrs. Zhu's left eye one Saturday at Glory Eye Center. The following Wednesday, I was taken to the countryside to visit her. I knew nothing of her story until I arrived at her home. There I discovered that Mrs. Zhu had only one son, and he had been in an accident eleven years before and had severed his spinal cord, leaving him unable to use his lower body. He had been bedridden since the accident.

After the accident, the son's wife left him and their two-year-old daughter. Unable to care for himself, let alone a two-year-old child, he was taken into his mother's one-room home. She was a widow and had no means of support, except for a very meager government subsidy, but she now became the sole caretaker of her invalid son and his infant child.

Though this life was very difficult, Mrs. Zhu gladly cared for her son and granddaughter — until, that is, she became blind with cataracts and could do it no longer. There was no facility in her rural village where she could have eye surgery performed, and she had no money to go into the city to get care. There were now three help-

With an elated lady who could now see to care for her paralyzed son, 1998.

The paralyzed son, so happy over his mother's recovery of sight, 1998.

158

Celebrating with a happy Chinese nurse
at the end of a day in surgery, 1998.

less people in one room, and they had no hope of changing their situation. The son and his mother had to begin to depend increasingly on the young child.

When we arrived at the little village, our car was surrounded by smiling villagers, among them a pretty young girl. She took my right hand in both of hers, like a ring bearer at a wedding might carry a precious ring on a small silk pillow, and led me down a small dirt pathway to a one-room house. As we got closer to the house, Mrs. Zhu came running out, talking animatedly and crying.

I had no idea who this young girl was or what Mrs. Zhu was saying. The interpreter told me that she was carrying on about how well she could see now. She was crying with gratitude and joy that she could now care for her son again and her granddaughter (the pretty

159

young girl who had led me to the house). All the village people were smiling and talking and making gestures, and they all seemed so happy that Mrs. Zhu could see again.

Mrs. Zhu took us inside her little house, where her son lay on the bed. He had crocheted a little red purse that he gave to me as a thank-you gift. I have it and treasure it to this day. Our gift of surgery and the miracle God did through our hands restored joy to the family and the entire village.

Mrs. Wang and I poured a great amount of time and effort and love and personal finances into helping people like these, but we soon found that there was only so much that a few individuals could do. This led to the creation of a program whereby people having a heart to help others could sponsor surgery for a poor person like Mrs. Zhu. Through a sponsor's gift of 2,000 RMB (about $250 U.S.), a blind person in China could be enabled to really live again.

A young Chinese couple had been saving money for their wedding and honeymoon. When they heard of this opportunity, they gave everything they had saved to make blind people see. In this way, our dream became contagious and developed a life of its own. It was all a result of God's love.

Until now, the dream is growing and gaining strength, until one day that Great Light will extinguish the darkness that shrouds the lives of millions of people today.

The following are selected excerpts from a few of the Chinese newspaper articles about Glory Eye Center.

Chapter 17

Excerpts from Chinese Newspaper Articles

From the time Glory Eye Center opened, there has been a stream of wonderful articles appearing in Chinese newspapers. Here are excerpts from a few of them:

LOVE: FROM THE OTHER SHORE OF THE OCEAN

An American ophthalmologist traveled to China ten times at her own expense. Those trips were not for pleasure, but to use her consummate medical skill to provide free surgery for poor people from deserted plateau areas. She came back to Beijing, China last month, with her scalpel and modern equipment, to complete her "Delivering Light with Loving Heart" international activity with Chinese eye experts. Her long-cherished wish is to enable more and more poor patients all over the world to see light again.

On May 21st there was a crowd at "Beijing Red Cross Glory Eye Center". In front of a big banner with "Dispel The Clouds and See The Light Again" on it, people were talking and inquiring with each other. They desperately yearned to be cured of their eye disease so they could see the world more clearly. They knew that a special doctor who came from America would do the exam and surgery for them. She is a famous doctor named Elizabeth Vaughan.

She arrived wearing a red dress and brown short hair. She was standing in front of the banner, giving a speech that touched everybody deeply in their hearts: "I've had a beautiful dream for a long time. I want to enable more and more poor patients all over the world to see light again. This is my eleventh visit to China for my dream." There was much applause by the crowd. Looking at those adoring patients who were suffering from eye diseases, her eyes brimmed with tears.

She started her work. The office with pink walls, green carpet, and flowers, looked more beautiful and peaceful because of her presence. She checked every patient's eyes very carefully. She did accurate, dexterous, and quick surgery for patients. At that time, it seemed there was a vehement love song playing in the quiet operating room. She got into the operating room at 8:30 a.m., and took a short break at 3:00 p.m. After having a hamburger, she went back to the operating room again and did surgery with Chinese doctors. When patients hugged her with tearful eyes, Dr. Vaughan always answered them with a tired smiling face. Words could not convey their gratitude.

Some doctors might not understand why a foreign doctor would give her heart to the poor patients and treat them for free. The story began four years ago. Elizabeth Vaughan, M.D., an eye expert who came from Dallas, U.S.A., was invited by Chinese Medical Scientist Academy to conduct modern surgical seminars in 1994. When she found out that thousands and thousands of people who lived in the poor areas were suffering from blindness, she started thinking about helping those patients with her consummate medical skill. As a result of this, she began to visit China more frequently at her own expense. She took her instruments and intraocular lenses, went to poor areas and did free surgery for patients by a modern technique called phacoemulsification. She earned high praise by the local citizens. She said: "There is no national boundaries of medical skill. I want to pass on my medical skills to Chinese doctors, teaching them to better serve people." For her dream, she visited Peking Union Medical College Hospital three times in recent years, conducting academic exchanges and giving surgical seminars. She did surgery for patients by herself. Everybody was deeply moved by her spirit. A patient remembered the scene when Dr. Vaughan did the surgery for her:

"October 12th, she had six cases of surgery scheduled. I was the last one. She was supposed to leave the next day. She did the surgeries one by one. It was 5:00 p.m. when she finished the first 5 patients. She had a meeting at 6:00 p.m., so there was no time for her to do my surgery. I had to go back to my ward. I was very disappointed. However, a few minutes later, I was told that Dr. Vaughan would do my surgery early the next morning. The next day, she came to the operating room very early with her assistants and did successful surgery for me. The surgery lasted until 9:30 a.m. She visited me before she went to the airport at noon."

Dr. Vaughan contributed her golden heart to the Chinese eye treatment cause and Chinese patients. Her "China's dream" is continuing. She wants to teach more and more Chinese doctors to master the modern techniques: removing a cataract by phacoemulsification in 10 minutes. She met Ms. Wang, an enthusiastic, smart, capable and experienced Chinese lady when she was working hard at finding a partner. Meanwhile, another warmhearted Chinese lady, Ms. Wang Chun Fang, the president of Alcon (China), Inc., got in touch with Dr. Vaughan. So one person's goal turned into three persons', and three turned into more and more. "Glory Eye Center" was born with the help of many people's loving hearts and Beijing Red Cross. The "Offering Love, Seeing Light" international activity was held by American and Chinese eye experts.

Dr. Vaughan brought light to Chinese patients. Her loving heart, consummate medical skill and her beautiful face have been branded in Chinese patients' hearts. "Glory Eye Center", which cements a profound friendship of China and America, will go down in history. More and more patients who walked in the darkness will now move toward the light with love.

[The article appeared with several photos of our work.]

 # CHINA DAILY

Vol. 18 No. 5440 Tuesday, February 17, 1998   Price: 80 fen; 90 fen (airmail)   http://www.chinadaily.n

[Under a photo of me working with a patient, and with several Chinese doctors looking on, the following appeared.]

Elizabeth Vaughan, an American doctor who cares about China's eye treatment cause, launches a 10-day voluntary diagnosis and operation seminar for eye patients yesterday at Guangming Eye Clinic, which is under the Beijing Red Cross Society. Together with eye experts from Beijing's Tongren and Union hospitals, she will also operate for free on those who are very poor.

CHINA WOMEN'S NEWS

1998 年 6 月 15 日 星期一   总第 2486 期 ■农历戊寅年五月廿一
国内统一刊号 CN11—0003(邮发代号 1—7)

FOREIGN ANGEL DELIVERS LIGHT
WITH SKILLFUL HANDS

Dr. Elizabeth R. Vaughan, M.D., an American ophthalmologist, came to China and saw patients at no cost during China's third "Loving Eyes Day".

The first time that Dr. Vaughan gave a modern surgical seminar in China was in 1994. At that time, she found out that thousands and thousands of patients who lived in the poor areas were suffering from blindness caused by cataracts, so she started thinking about helping those patients voluntarily. As a result of this, she began to visit China more frequently. She took her own instruments and intraocular lens, traveling at her own expense to the poor areas, such as Gan Gu, treating eye disease by using the most modern technique, phacoemulsification. She will do free surgery for 10 patients who are very poor during the "Loving Eyes Day" activity.

[Several photos with captions accompanied the article.]

165

ANGEL THAT BRINGS LIGHT

People always say to love your life like you love your eyes. It is thus clear that eyes are extremely important to people. But many factors, especially eye disease, can cause blindness. Cataract is the worst menace among numerous diseases. There are over 40,000,000 cataract patients in China.

Faced with the arduous task of preventing and curing blindness, "Glory Eye Center" offers a high standard of eye care in China. It was established by Beijing Red Cross and a famous American ophthalmologist, Elizabeth R. Vaughan, M.D. "Glory Eye Center" is located in Song yu li, Chao yao district, Beijing. It is an ophthalmology clinic, treating common eye diseases such as cataract, glaucoma, and myopia. After visiting "Glory Eye Center", a famous government official of China said with feeling to the American and Chinese doctors: "You are angels that bring light to Chinese people".

[This article appeared with a lovely photo of our surgical crew.]

日报 今日共16版 ■1998 年 2 月 12 日■星期四■第 3428 期■统一刊号：CN 11 – 0103 ■ 国 外 发 行 代 号 ：D 1253 ■

AN AMERICAN EYE EXPERT LAUNCHES VOLUNTARY DIAGNOSIS IN BEIJING — A LONG MARCH OF 5 THOUSAND KILOMETERS, BECAUSE OF DEEP AFFECTION OF PATIENTS

Elizabeth R. Vaughan, M.D., an American ophthalmologist who is sympathetic to China's eye treatment cause, will come to Beijing conducting academic exchanges, giving surgical seminars, and doing free surgery for patients who are blind and very poor. She will see patients free, together with eye experts from Beijing Tongren Hospital, Peking Union Medical College Hospital and Beijing Medical University Hospital for 1 week at "Glory Eye Center".

"Glory Eye Center", which will be opened in the next few days, is achieving good results treating eye diseases such as cataract, glaucoma and myopia by modern techniques and equipment. All doctors of "Glory Eye Center" have M.D. or Master's degrees, over 10 years working experience and professional training in the U.S. They are good at treating eye diseases. It takes only 10 minutes to remove a cataract by phacoemulsification. Patients will recover in the second day after surgery without being in the hospital.

MEDCINE & FOODS

人民日报社 主办

1998 年 2 月 6 日

第 42 期

互联网络网址：http∥www. snweb. com

ANGEL THAT BRINGS LIGHT

Elizabeth R. Vaughan, M.D., who came from Texas, U.S.A, is a very experienced eye surgeon. She has mastered the modern techniques. She conducted academic exchanges, gave lectures, and gave surgical seminars several times in Beijing and Shanghai. She has been doing phacoemulsification surgery for cataracts almost 25 years and has done over 8,000 cases of radial keratotomy surgery for nearsightedness. She has accumulated a wealth of experience in eye surgery. She plans to come to "Glory Eye Center" to do surgery every year. The first time for her to come to "Glory Eye Center" is from Feb. 14th to Feb. 27th this year. Showing the love from Dr. Vaughan and all the staff of "Glory Eye Center", they will see patients free and offer free cataract surgery with intraocular lens insertion for needy patients who are very poor.

SEEING LIGHT AGAIN ON "LOVING EYES DAY"

Dr. Elizabeth R. Vaughan, M.D., an American ophthalmologist, held a consulting service and saw patients at no cost, together with ten eye experts from other hospitals at "Glory Eye Center" on China's third "Loving Eyes Day" in Beijing. Dr. Vaughan did free surgery for two patients who are very poor on that day.

[A photo was included of me supporting an elderly patient, Ms. Liu xiu Qing, as she walked out of the operating room.]

ANGEL THAT BRINGS LIGHT

"Glory Eye Center" has not only superb technique, but also has the modern equipment which is advanced in China and overseas.

We hope more and more people who are eager to see the light can enjoy the beautiful life in the world with the help of "Glory Eye Center".

AMERICAN EYE EXPERT WILL SEE NEEDY PATIENTS FREE IN BEIJING

Elizabeth R. Vaughan, M.D., an American ophthalmologist who is invited by Beijing Red Cross, Beijing Committee of Prevention and Cure of Chronic Disease, and Beijing Committee of Prevention of Blindness, will come to Beijing conducting academic exchanges, operation seminars, and doing free surgery for patients who are very poor from Feb. 16th to Feb. 26. She will see needy patients at no charge. Other eye experts will join her at "Glory Eye Center" for 1 week.

Chapter 18

The First Mobile Unit

In an attempt to reach more and more of those in need, we began sending teams into the countryside every week from Glory Eye Center. Each team included an opthalmologist, an eye nurse and other ancillary personnel. They would carry examination equipment from the center, and this was cumbersome, but essential to the task. Hundreds of poor people would be screened and treated and the very worst ones would be brought into Beijing for surgery.

The ideal way to reach the rural people, we had long-ago discovered, would be to have mobile examination units and mobile surgery units to take to areas of great need, so that far more poor people could be helped. With mobile units, we could reach areas much farther away from Beijing, and we had noticed that the needs increased greatly the farther one traveled from the big cities. Not only were the poor in those areas unable to afford care, no care was available to them. We had seen people permanently blinded, time and time again, from glaucoma, which can be cured through a simple surgical procedure or a laser treatment. It broke my heart to see people totally and permanently blinded by something I could have cured them of in ten minutes with proper equipment.

Each of us can imagine how we would feel if this happened to our mother or someone else we love — or even to us personally. Most of us would spend every last dollar we have to keep from going blind.

I was compelled to press forward with more help for these poor people.

In the summer of 1999, I was again taken to the countryside, to the home of a man who had undergone surgery at Glory Eye Center. He was elderly and poor, living in one room with his wife. About a third of the space in the small room was taken up by a mud bed. These are common in rural areas of China where bedding is unaffordable and where it is cold. A slab is made of mud and allowed to harden. Mats of straw are then placed over the hard mud and the people lie on the mats. The ingenious feature of the apparatus is the heater. A small black potbellied stove is vented into the space under the mud slab, and this provides warmth for the family as they sleep during the cold winter nights.

Though advanced in years, this man would ride his bicycle several miles to a factory, where he still worked part-time to earn enough money to support himself and his wife. He also had a small vegetable garden in front of his one-room home, where he could grow food for the two of them. They were getting by on this subsistence income — until his vision began to fail. It got worse and worse, until he could neither see well enough to ride his bicycle to work nor to work in his vegetable garden. Life had closed in on him and created a dark world with very little activity and no hope of improvement.

Then one day the Glory Eye Center team came to his village and someone led him to a screening area. His heart leaped for joy, and he dared entertain a small ray of hope for the future.

Yes, he was told, they could help him and they would. He was transported to Beijing where Dr. Joe did cataract surgery on him free of charge. When I arrived at his home, he was "all smiles," and a television crew was on hand to capture his joy and his appreciation.

The man demonstrated for us how he could again ride his bicycle and see where he was going. His little garden was already beginning to show signs of new life because he could now see to care for it. As I stood there listening to him bubble on in Chinese (which I could not understand), the Spirit of the Lord spoke to me and said, "When you have done it unto one of the least of these, you have done it unto Me." Tears filled my eyes as I realized that, from God's perspective, operating on that poor, elderly Chinese man was the same as operating on Jesus. We would continue to run this race with all our might and not look back.

Mrs. Wang said they had a big surprise for me on June 6, 1999. Every year, on June 6, the Chinese celebrate "Love Your Eyes Day," and she had prepared a big celebration at Glory Eye Center. The dancing ladies in red were back and so were the speeches over the loudspeakers in the streets and the crowds watching it all. The big surprise, however, turned out to be a brand-new customized van, our first mobile examination unit.

It was built tough enough to pass over the bad or barely existent roads in rural areas, yet it had heat for the winter and air-conditioning for the summer. With this unit, we could greatly expand our operations.

It had a lighted eye chart for vision testing, and stools and tables for examination purposes were bolted to the floor so they would not topple over when the unit was in motion. The cabin area had a second bench-type seat behind the driver, so the doctors and nurse could have a place to sit comfortably while traveling to rural areas.

The unit was white and oh so beautiful. Mrs. Wang had placed a big red ribbon around the front of the vehicle with a huge red bow in the center. We had a ribbon-cutting ceremony, with the head of the Beijing Red Cross, Mrs. Wang and myself doing the honors.

Immediately after the celebration had ended, we headed to the countryside and began screening and treating poor people. What a glorious day! Our dream of Glory Eye Center had been fulfilled

With Dr. Zhang and Mrs. Wang at the dedication of the mobile examination unit, 1999.

The first mobile examination unit.

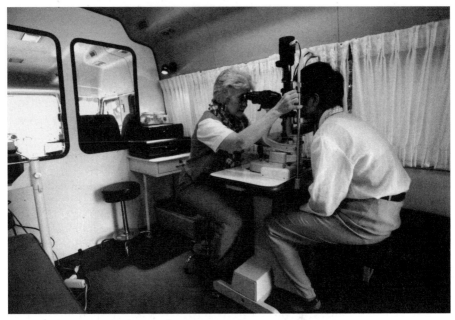

Examining a patient inside the mobile examination unit, June 1999.

Patients waiting to be seen in the mobile examination unit in rural China, June 1999.

the year before, and now our first mobile eye examination unit had been launched.

The next step would be a mobile surgery unit, which would be more involved and more expensive than the examination unit, because it would require running water, a generator, an operating microscope and many other surgical instruments. When I asked Mrs. Wang how we had gotten the money for the mobile examination unit, she said that one of her friends had donated the funds for it. This donor and all those who are sponsoring surgery for the blind may not realize it as yet, but they are being used as instruments in God's hands.

The River Disco

Mrs. Wang loves to have parties and do karaoke. This is where the guests, either individually or in groups, get up and sing songs with background music, and the words are projected onto a screen so that everyone can sing along if they like. She has a huge library of karaoke songs in both Chinese and English. Just before I left Beijing after one of our trips, she had a big farewell party, inviting all the staff of Glory Eye Center, plus quite a number of other important Chinese people. After a scrumptious dinner in a room with a big wooden dance floor, she turned on the karaoke machine and started asking people to perform.

Ability has nothing to do with these performances. Practically no one has a good voice, but everyone is expected to participate. I put off my turn as long as possible, but finally I had to do it. So I asked Geri and Deborah to come with me. We selected "The Yellow Rose of Texas," which we barely knew, and got up on the stage by the dance floor for our "performance." No one fell out of their chairs laughing, so I guess our song was passable.

When we finished singing, I had the bright idea of teaching them all an Israeli dance. I got everyone up on the dance floor and had them form a big circle. We all joined hands, and I started singing a lively, but simple, song in Hebrew and showing them how to kick their legs in time with the music. They all participated, but no one seemed to really "get into it," like we were accustomed to doing in America.

In a few minutes, someone turned on a rotating multi-mirrored ball on the ceiling that was reflecting bits of light all over the poorly-lit dance floor. Simultaneously, loud disco music came on, and everyone started dancing, either alone or with a partner. Deborah, Geri and I stood there looking startled. There we were in the middle of the dance floor, with people dancing wildly all around us, and we had no idea of how to do this dance.

We thought it might be considered rude to go sit down, when we were the honored guests, and everyone else was out there dancing vigorously. Just at that moment, I remembered a little dance I learned in a crusade once where we would sing a song about swimming in the river (of the Holy Ghost) and at the same time make swimming motions with our arms. Everyone in the church would sing this song and "swim" in that glorious river. So I looked at Deborah and Geri, who were standing there like stone monuments, and I said, "Let's swim in the river." A smile came on their faces, and the three of us began "swimming" in time to the music. We would twirl around and do a little backstroke, then a little breaststroke, and then a little "crawl."

We were each dancing alone, since no one else had ever seen this, but pretty soon one of the young Chinese doctors came over in front of me and started doing the swiming motions too. I guess he thought it was some new and wonderful American dance that he wanted to learn. I started laughing as I "swam," because the whole thing was hilarious. I guess he thought I was having a really good time, "dancing" with him, so he did his gyrations even more vigorously. Others started doing swimming motions also since we seemed to be having so much fun. It was really a funny sight.

Deborah and Geri and I danced in the river of God so long and with so much joy that night that we really did have a good time. I guess somewhere in Beijing tonight people are doing the new American dance we taught them — swimming in the river. No one can ever say the Holy Spirit does not have a sense of humor.

Chapter 19

The Picture

One day I watched a famous Chinese painter working with black ink and various-sized brushes. He started with a large blank piece of white paper, selected a brush and began making strokes. Some strokes were darker, and some were lighter. Some were made slowly and carefully, while others were sweeping and masterful. Some were very broad, and others were paper thin. I looked at the accumulation of strokes as he worked, and I could not tell what his final painting would be. No visible image appeared. His many and varied lines looked disjointed, meaning nothing.

None of us who watched that day could guess what the final picture was going to be, but the master painter knew what he was doing. He had the picture he wanted to make in his mind; he had it in his heart; and it would eventually come out through his hand onto the paper.

The strokes continued, and there was a hush of anticipation and wonder, as everyone watched this master at work. We were all sure that the end result would have meaning and form and beauty, but none of us could see it yet. It was still within the master and not yet in plain view.

After working quite a while, the painter finally began to connect the strokes, and as he connected them, suddenly we could see a ti-

179

Painting a picture with "strokes." What will emerge? 1998.

ger emerging in all his grandeur. The tiger had been in the mind and heart of the painter all along, but it was now on the paper for all of us to see.

We are now in the middle of the picture God is painting for China. He is making masterful strokes, but we cannot see the final product yet. We are happy and content in knowing that we are in His hand, being used by Him. How He chooses to use us is not in our control; it is in God's control. Even if the strokes do not make any sense to us at the moment, it is all right, because we live by the advice God gave us:

> *Trust in the LORD with all thine heart; and lean not unto thine own understanding. In all thy ways acknowledge him, and he shall direct thy paths.*   Proverbs 3:5-6

We know with certainty that God is loving the Chinese people through us. We know that He is serving the people and taking care of their desperate needs by making blind people see. He is building a strong platform of love and trust as we continue to return many, many times over the years. And we know that someday, in His timing and in His all-knowing way, He will openly pour forth the power of the resurrected Jesus Christ on His Chinese children. He is the only one that can do this, for it is, *"Not by might, nor by power, but by my spirit, saith the LORD of hosts"* (Zechariah 4:6).

He has promised through His prophets:

> *For the earth shall be filled with the knowledge of the glory of the LORD, as the waters cover the sea.* Habakkuk 2:14

We thoroughly expect to be in China and be used by God as vessels to pour out His glory on our beloved Chinese. We will be vessels they trust, because they know WE LOVE THEM and have only brought good to them over the years in a selfless way.

When in China, I always wear a jade cross around my neck everywhere I go, even in surgery. The Chinese people know without a word that that cross means I love Jesus, I am His servant, and I come in His name. They may know nothing whatsoever about Jesus, but they have to assume from our works that He is filled with love and a caring nature.

One blind lady held my hand and said, "I can't see you with my eyes, but I can feel you with my heart." The love of Jesus is often conveyed without words.

On several occasions, I have been asked to speak to hospital staffs, not about eye surgery, but about "how to treat patients." By this, the head of the hospital doesn't mean medicine at all. He wants me to teach his staff how to be kind and gentle with patients, how to treat

Teaching a hospital staff in China, 1998.

the patients the way the staff would want to be treated if they were sick and afraid. Instead of being curt and impatient, as busy people sometimes are, he wants his staff to be taught patience and a caring nature. Without saying the name of Jesus, His love and His virtue is being transferred into these hospitals.

So I don't lean on my own understanding, which is far too small. I trust Him to fulfill the work that is in His heart with the instruments He has in His hand. And when the Master Painter is through with the picture in China, it will not be a picture of a tiger, but rather a picture of a Lion, the Lion of the tribe of Judah, whose name is JESUS.

The World

Over the years, God has sent me to many other countries. My cup overflows with memories — like crossing the Russian border in the middle of the night in a green Volkswagon van, praying for a Zulu witch doctor in South Africa, and trudging through a slushy rain forest in Costa Rica with a missionary friend. There are too many experiences to relate in this volume, but I have included a few photos here to share with you from my life and my travels.

Praying for a Zulu witch doctor in South Africa, 1985.

With Dr. Fyodorov, the famous Russian ophthalmologist who developed radial keratotomy, 1987.

Friends that work with me in surgery: Elaine (my circulating nurse), Dr. Garcia (my anesthesiologist) and Dottie (my scrub nurse), 1989.

Praying for the sick in Costa Rica, 1994.

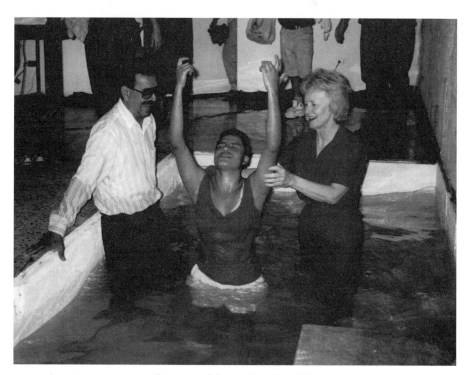

Baptizing new believers in Costa Rica, 1994.

Receiving a gift from the church after the crusade in Costa Rica, 1994.

With a missionary friend in the rain forest of Costa Rica, 1994.

Chapter 20

Ordinary People As Instruments in God's Hand

One thing I want us all to see as we reflect back on these China experiences is that God uses people as instruments in what we might consider ordinary things. As we go through our usual workdays, God's hand is on us. Too many times we think that God only uses instruments in a church, a synagogue, or some other religious edifice. That is very far from the truth. Obviously God does use instruments in His house, but He also uses them in the ordinary paths of life.

Think of the life of Jesus. He was usually out of doors or in someone's home when miracles were done or words of life were spoken. Like Jesus, God will use us in the same ordinary places, in our homes, or where we work, or walking down the street or in a restaurant. He most commonly uses ordinary people, in ordinary places, doing ordinary things, as instruments in His hand. So in China, whether we were in surgery or walking through an open-air market or playing ping-pong, God could still use us as instruments, and He can do the same with you.

A plumber comes to mind who was called to a motel room to fix the sink. In that room was an evangelist who was burnt out and about ready to quit the ministry. That plumber, in the middle of an ordinary workday, led the evangelist into the baptism of the Holy Spirit in that motel room, saving that man's ministry and setting him on fire for God. We need to change our concept of instruments and realize that WE ARE instruments today, right now, right where God planted us.

Jesus said:

> *And this gospel of the kingdom shall be preached in all the world*
> *for a witness unto all nations; and then shall the end come.*
>
> Matthew 24:14

This world of ours needs major surgery. The Great Physician, Jesus, has donned His surgical gown, with His hat, mask and gloves. He is poised and ready to start the operation with us as His instruments, yielded, available and ready for His use.

The stage is set for the world to watch as the Holy Spirit accomplishes this seemingly impossible operation with speed and dexterity and ease. He *will* make the Bride of Christ ready; He *will* gather in all of those who will come; He *will* make Jesus Christ known and worshiped on a grand scale worldwide. The task is not difficult for the all-powerful Holy Spirit. He has just been waiting for the Father to say, "It is time."

And when the operation is finished, the sky will split open, and Jesus will motion for us to come home, saying, "Well done My good and faithful instruments. Enter into the joy of the Lord."

— THE END —

There is really no limit to what God can do with a person, providing that one will not touch the glory. God is still waiting for one who will be more fully devoted to Him than any who has ever lived; who will be willing to be nothing that Christ may be all; who will grasp God's own purposes and taking His humility and His faith, His love and His power — without hindering, let God do great things.   Kathryn Kuhlman

(from a letter to Dr. Vaughan dated January, 1975)

Ministry address:

Elizabeth R. Vaughan, M.D.
P.O. Box 191772
Dallas, TX 75219